1000
MILITARY AIRCRAFT
IN COLOUR

1000
MILITARY AIRCRAFT
IN COLOUR

GERRY MANNING

Airlife
England

Copyright © 2001 Gerry Manning

First published in the UK in 2001
by Airlife Publishing Ltd

British Library Cataloguing-in-Publication Data
A catalogue record for this book
is available from the British Library

ISBN 1 84037 199 4

Typeset by Echelon, Wimborne
Printed in China

Airlife Publishing Ltd
101 Longden Road, Shrewsbury, SY3 9EB, England
E-mail: airlife@airlifebooks.com
Website: www.airlifebooks.com

ACKNOWLEDGEMENTS

I would like to thank the four contributors of pictures who have been able to fill in some of the gaps in my own collection. They are, in alphabetical order, Phil Duckett (P.J.D.), Tony Griffiths (A.G.), John Smith (J.D.S.) and Steve Williams (S.G.W.). Photographs without a credit are my own.

INTRODUCTION

This is a military companion for my 1998 book, *1000 Airlines in Colour*. It shows the range of military aeroplanes and the colour schemes worn. The aim is not just to look at the latest fast jets, they are in, but to show the range of aircraft types that have served in uniform over the last forty years.

Military aircraft have in recent years been lasting longer and longer in service. Who would have believed that when the B-52 first flew in 1952 it would not only still be in service today but scheduled to continue until 2020. This example is now only one of many.

The colour schemes on a lot of military aircraft types today can be described as grey with grey markings. These are a far cry from the dazzling colours on some of the older aircraft illustrated. An effort has been made to show examples of the special markings that squadrons apply for anniversaries to help bring some colour to the pages of the newest types.

The order of the pictures is: fighters and bombers then trainers, transport including assorted liaison designs, maritime, helicopters and, to end, a section of aerobatic teams. These sortings are only approximate, as so many aircraft are now multi-role some could fit in almost any category. Where types have different functions they are grouped together for ease of comparison.

It must be accepted by the reader that there is a long time lapse between finishing the text and it being published. I have tried to keep it as up to date as possible but some things will have changed during this time period. An index of aircraft types is included at the back of the book.

Gerry Manning
Liverpool

Right: The MiG-25 was designed to combat the menace, to the Russians, of the North American XB70 Valkyrie, a high-flying Mach-3 bomber. The Americans cancelled the project but the MiG went ahead. The fighter, with a 3,000 km/hr speed together with its bulk, it was 71 ft 6 in (22.3 m) long with a wing span of 45 ft 2 in (14.1 m), was not a dogfighter. It was also used as a reconnaissance platform. Illustrated is 01(Blue) a **MiG-25U-LL**. Note that the rear seat is open as this airframe is used to test ejector seats at high speeds. It is seen at its base, Zhukovsky, in August 1995.

Above: Pictured is 91(Red) a **MiG-25PU**. This is a two-seat training version, note how the extra place has been grafted onto the nose section. It is seen taxiing out to take off at the Russian research base at Zhukovsky, August 1995.

Below: The current backbone of the Swedish Air Force (*Flygvapnet*) is the multi-role **SAAB 37 Viggen** (Thunderbolt). Seen visiting Finningley in September 1986 is 37330 a JA37 of F13; this variant is configured as a fighter.

Above: The **SAAB 39 Gripen** (Griffin) is the latest design from the Swedish manufacturer. It is a true multi-role machine, being a fighter, an attack and a reconnaissance aircraft in one. Seen at Farnborough, is JAS39 39.4, September 1992.

Above: Sweden has for many years had a 'go it alone' policy with the design and manufacture of very advanced warplanes. This complements the national neutral status. In October 1955 they first flew the Mach-2 interceptor, the **SAAB 35 Draken** (Dragon). The first production aircraft were delivered towards the end of that decade. Seen here at its Angelholm base, August 1995, is 35586 62/F10, a **J35J** variant. F10 was the last unit to operate the type in front-line service. (PJD)

Right: The Finnish Air Force is in the process of replacing its Draken fleet with F/A18 Hornets. Seen at Pirkkala, part of Satakunta Air Command, is **J35FS Draken** DK263, a single-seat interceptor of HaLLv 21, June 1998. The unit was in transition at this time.

Left: DK270 is a **SAAB Sk35CS Draken** two-seat trainer of HaLLv 11 (11th Fighter Squadron) of the Finnish Air Force (*Soumen Ilmaviomat*). It is seen at its base, Rovaniemi on the Arctic Circle, June 1998. The unit is part of Lapland Air Command.

Below: Denmark was the only NATO country to operate the Swedish double delta. AR110, an **S35XD Draken** of Esk 729, is seen in its all-over green scheme at Upper Heyford, June 1984. These aircraft have been replaced by F16s.

Above: The **North American F86 Sabre** has had a long service life. Land-locked Bolivia must have been the last front-line user with three airframes being operated as late as 1992. Seen here in November of that year is F86F FAB658 of *Grupo Aereo de Caza* 32 at its base of El Trompillo, Santa Cruz de la Sierra.

Left: The Sabre was built under licence in Canada, and the main difference from the North American machines was the powerplant. An Avro Orenda from the Sabre 3 was used instead of the General Electric J47. **Sabre 6** 23459 in the markings of 421 Squadron, 2 Wing, Royal Canadian Air Force is seen at Prestwick in May 1963. (AG)

Above: Scottish Aviation serviced many military aircraft. Seen here is 23664, a Canadian **Sabre 6** of 444 (Cobra) Squadron RCAF, 2 Wing, from West Germany at Prestwick, May 1963. (AG)

Above: The popular image of **F86 Sabres** in service with the United States Air Force is that of silver airframes with colourful squadron markings. However, during the last few years of service camouflage was applied to some aircraft. Pictured is **F86H** 53-1506 of the 104th Fighter Squadron, Maryland Air National Guard. It is seen at Pittsburgh in August 1970, the month the type was replaced by the Cessna A37B. (SGW)

Below: The sad fate of many military aircraft is to be a target. **Canadair Sabre 5** 23320/N74170 is seen at Mojave, CA, October 1979, during service with the US Army. It was re-designated as a QF86E and this airframe was shot down over the White Sands Missile Range in New Mexico in August the following year.

Above: **QF86H Sabre** 53-1409 is a target drone operated by the US Navy at its China Lake test centre. It was seen at Edwards AFB in October 1979.

Below: The French answer to the Eurofighter is the Dassault Rafale. It is designed to be both a land-based fighter for the French Air Force and a naval version to operate from the French Navy aircraft carriers. The first prototype 01 is seen at the Farnborough Air Show in September 1988.

Above: The shape of things to come is seen here with Eurofighter 2000 ZH588. The aircraft is a joint project of Britain, Germany, Italy and Spain, all of whom will build parts of the aircraft and operate the type within their own air forces. This BaeSystems operated prototype is seen at Farnborough in September 1996. The Royal Air Force plans to operate a total of 232 with options on a further sixty-five. The first deliveries to the Operational Evaluation Unit will be in 2002.

Above: The Supermarine Scimitar F1 was a Royal Navy–Fleet Air Arm single-seat strike/fighter, powered by two Rolls-Royce Avon 202 turbojets of 11,250 lb static thrust. First flown in January 1957, the first operational squadron (803) formed in June the following year. XD228 613 of 736 Squadron is seen at Brawdy, July 1963. (AG)

Above: Scimitar F1 XD219 is seen at RNAS Brawdy in August 1968. It is on charge to the Naval Aircraft Servicing Unit (NASU) at that location.

Above: The Gloster Javelin was a two-seat delta wing all-weather fighter equipped with radar and four de Havilland Firestreak air-to-air missiles. In February 1956, 46 Squadron equipped with Javelin FAW1s which were the first in service. Last of the line was the illustrated XH897, an FAW9. It is on charge to the A&AEE (Aeroplane and Armament Experimental Establishment) at Boscombe Down. It was photographed in September 1971 at Coltishall.

Above: The Dassault Mystere IV.A was first flown in September 1952. It served with the French as well as the air forces of India and Israel. No. 295 is seen at Sculthorpe, in May 1976, in the markings of ET 2/8 'Nice'. Coded 8-NA, it carries the black and white stork badge of the unit on the fin top.

Below: Israel Aircraft Industries designed the Kfir which is based upon the Mirage 5. It is powered by a single General Electric J79 engine, giving a Mach 2 performance, and is used as an interceptor and ground attack aircraft. Kfir C2 779/4XCFL is seen at the Paris Air Show, June 1977.

Above: The Dassault Super Mystere B2 was a supersonic single-seat interceptor and fighter-bomber. Seen at Upper Heyford, in June 1971, is No. 88 of EC 1/12 'Cambresis' coded 12-YD. It has a tiger's head on the fin and is the regular *Armée de l'Air* participant at NATO Tiger Meets.

Below: The de Havilland Sea Venom entered service with the Royal Navy in 1954. It was the service's first all-weather jet fighter. By the end of that decade they were being replaced by the same manufacturer's Sea Vixen. Following this they soldiered on in second-line duties. The Air Director Training Unit at RNAS Yeovilton operates Sea Venom FAW22 XG729 733/VL. It is seen at Chivenor in August 1969.

Above: With a service life of nearly forty years in the Swedish Air Force, the last use of the SAAB 32 Lansen was as an electronic warfare training aircraft. 32512 J32E 03/F16M is seen visiting Fairford in July 1994 from its base at Malmslätt.

Below: Seen here in an all-white non-standard colour scheme is A&AEE de Havilland Sea Vixen FAW1 XJ476 at its home base Boscombe Down, March 1971. The Sea Vixen was the Fleet Air Arm's first swept wing all-weather, two-seat interceptor. The nose of this aircraft is preserved at the Southampton Hall of Aviation.

Below: Many of the Sea Vixen FAW1s were converted to FAW2 standard. This later variant had extra fuel capacity by the extension of the booms forward together with the launch system for the air-to-air Red Top missile. XJ521, coded 705/VL, is operated by 766 Squadron at RNAS Yeovilton. It is seen at Chivenor in August 1969. 766 was the type's training unit. The design was to be replaced within three years when the F4 Phantom entered service.

Below: As the Soviet Union began to build a 'blue water' navy they had to start from scratch to operate aircraft carriers and the aircraft that flew from them. The Yakovlev Yak-38 (NATO code-name Forger) was the first practical VTOL aircraft to fly off the carrier *Kiev*. The aircraft had a main engine with two extra lift engines. Seen hovering at Zhukovsky, in August 1995, is 24(Yellow) a Yak-38U two-seat trainer. The extra nose area makes this perhaps one of the most ugly aeroplanes flying today.

Above: Flight Refuelling at Tarrent Rushton converted a small number of Sea Vixens to pilotless drone targets with the designation D3. XS587 is at Valley, in August 1983, on charge to the RAE. The drone program moved ahead very slowly and finally closed down.

Right: NATO code-name Freestyle, the Yakovlev Yak-141 was to have been the next generation of VTOL fighter on the Soviet Navy's carriers. The end of communism has found the Russian Republic short of funds to develop defence projects. 141(White) is at Zhukovsky, August 1995. The type is very unlikely to achieve any quantity production.

Below: The MiG (Mikoyan & Gurevich) 31 had its roots in the MiG-25, however with its phased array radar system and very long-range air-to-air missiles it is a far more efficient interceptor. **MiG-31M** 057(Blue) is seen under power at Zhukovsky, August 1995. This aircraft was the seventh and final 31M, the most advanced variant; it has electronic warfare pods on the wing tips. Code-named Foxhound by NATO, the decline in the Russian defence budgets is likely to see that this is the last version of the type.

Above: With a Mach 2+ performance the swing-wing MiG-23 (NATO code-name Flogger) was one of the most widely used interceptors in the Soviet Air Force and the states within their sphere of influence. 56(Red) is a **MiG-23UB** two-seat trainer taxiing to take off at Zhukovsky, in August 1995. The emblem on the nose is not a squadron badge but a device to scare birds.

Above: Towing its drag chute is Russian **MiG-23UB** 64(Red) of 296 APIB at its then, base at Grossenhain, July 1992. This airfield was in the old German Democratic Republic and like all such locations the Russians have moved out and back east. (PJD)

Below: Papa in Hungary is the location of this **MiG-23MF** (Flogger B) of the *Magyar Legiero* – Hungarian Air Force – 47th Tactical Fighter Wing. 08(Red) was photographed in September 1997. (PJD)

Above: Seen landing at Fairford, July 1997, is the Czech Air Force's **MiG-23ML** 2425 of 41SLT. The type has since been withdrawn from service as the Czechs look forward to western equipment after joining NATO in 1999.

Above: Seen on the ramp at Constanta-Mikhail Kogalnicanu is Romanian Air Force **MiG-23MF** 224 of the 57th Regiment. Note the difference in colours for the different roles from the same unit's MiG-29. The aircraft was photographed in May 1999. (PJD)

Below: The **Mirage 111S** is the Swiss variant and has features such as better brakes and a tail hook to cope with some of the shorter Swiss airfields. J2325 in the original bare metal is seen at Dübendorf, August 1987. It carries the badge of FlSt 17 who are based at Payerne.

Above: For France the Dassault Mirage 111 series of aircraft was one of the most successful ever. Besides the home market they were sold to many countries including Israel. The 'Six Day War' in 1967 was the combat seal of approval. The illustrated example is No. 346 a **Mirage 111R** 33-CO of *Escadre de Reconnaisance* ER1/33 'Belfort'. The unit badge is a battle-axe, as seen on the fin. It is seen at Châteaudun, June 1977.

Below: The Mirage 111RS is the photo reconnaissance variant of the type, note the different shape of the nose. R-2104 of Swiss Air Force unit *Fliegerstaffel* 10 is pictured at the unit's base in Dübendorf, August 1987.

Above: The new colour of so many military aeroplanes today is grey. In an air defence grey is Swiss Air Force Mirage 111S J-2311 at Dübendorf, August 1987.

Below: Seen visiting Edwards AFB in October 1979, is Oregon ANG F101B Voodoo 58-0329 of the 123rd FIS. The unit flew this design for ten years starting in 1971.

Below: Built by McDonnell (later McDonnell Douglas and now Boeing) the F101 Voodoo was built to be a fighter with SAC (Strategic Air Command) and went on to serve with most USAF commands. It was also operated by the Canadian and Chinese Nationalists. 58-0261 F101B of the 2nd FITS is seen landing at its base at Tyndall, FL, October 1981.

Below: Texas, the lone star state, operated F101F Voodoos. The 'F' variant was a reworked 'B' with an improved fire control and infra-red detection systems. These replaced the in-flight refuelling probe. 58-0276 is seen visiting Eglin AFB, Florida, in October 1981, and is operated by 111th Fighter Squadron, Texas ANG.

Below: A reconfigured nose shows this aircraft to be a photo reconnaissance version of the Voodoo. RF101C 56-0112 is operated by the 66th TRW, which was based at Upper Heyford during the period this picture was taken. It was photographed at RAF Valley in August 1968, in the camouflage colours worn at this time.

Below: Showing off what the colours used to be is F101A Voodoo 54-1455, seen at Alconbury, May 1964. It displays the multi-coloured tail of the 81st TFW then based at Bentwaters. It is of note that one of the weapons carried by the Voodoo was the MB-1 Genie air-to-air missile with a nuclear warhead; a near miss would still manage to destroy the target! (AG)

Above: Seen at its home base RNAS Brawdy, in July 1962, is Hawker Sea Hawk FGA6 XE340 124/C of 801 Squadron. The 'C' code is for its carrier base HMS *Centaur*. The Sea Hawk entered service with 806 Squadron in March 1953; this particular aircraft has survived and is in a museum at Montrose in Scotland. (AG)

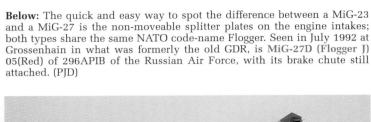

Below: The quick and easy way to spot the difference between a MiG-23 and a MiG-27 is the non-moveable splitter plates on the engine intakes; both types share the same NATO code-name Flogger. Seen in July 1992 at Grossenhain in what was formerly the old GDR, is **MiG-27D (Flogger J)** 05(Red) of 296APIB of the Russian Air Force, with its brake chute still attached. (PJD)

Above: NATO gave the code-name 'Fitter' to the range of Sukhoi ground attack fighters starting with the Su-7. The final 'Fitter' variant is the **Su-22M-4**. The quickest recognition point is the ram air inlet at the base of the tail fin. 4007 (Fitter K) code 32 of 32ZTL Czech Air Force is at Fairford, July 1995.

Below: An action shot of **Sukhoi Su-22M-4** 4007 as it lands at Fairford, in July 1995, with another (3802) of the same type behind it.

Above: Avro Canada designed and built the CF100, a two-seat all-weather fighter. A subsonic straight-wing aeroplane, it was also operated by the Belgian Air Force. 18358 **CF100 Mk4B** in the colours of 423 AW(F) (All Weather Fighter) squadron is seen at Prestwick, May 1963. (AG)

Right: Republic's **F105 Thunderchief** was an all-weather strike fighter. The type bore the brunt of the air war over North Vietnam for many years of that conflict. **F105D** 61-0093 is seen at Lakenheath in October 1976, at the end of a line of aircraft from the 121st TFS/113th FW District of Columbia ANG.

Left: To combat the growing menace of the ground-to-air missile, a number of Thunderchiefs (54) were converted to 'Wild Weasel' missile suppression standard. These were two-seat aircraft and armed with anti-radiation (radar) missiles. **F105G** 63-8320 WW/35th TFW is seen at home base in George AFB, CA, October 1979. This aircraft shot down a MiG-17 over North Vietnam on 19 December 1967. It is also credited with two further MiG kills and has been preserved by the USAF museum.

Below: France's current front-line fighter is the **Mirage 2000**. A Chimera (Dragon) is on the fin of this 2000B No. 510 2-FG of ECT 2/2, which was photographed at Conningsby, in June 1989.

Above: In order to train pilots to fly the big F105 a two-seat variant was produced. Seen here is **F105F**, 62-4414 operated by 149th TFS/192nd TFG Virginia ANG, with both cockpits open. It was photographed during a visit to Lakenheath in October 1976.

Left: Based at Keflavik, Iceland the 57th FIS operated the **Convair F102 Delta Dagger** from 1964 to 1973. The location assured that the 'Black Knights', as the squadron was known, were at the sharp end of many intercepts of Russian aircraft over the north Atlantic. **F102A** 56-1418 is seen on a visit to Leuchars to uplift fuel, September 1972.

Below: One of the features of the Delta Dagger was that it was a complete weapons system with an internal weapons bay. Its development was long and protracted. The type gave excellent service as an interceptor in the various Air National Guard units. **F102A** 56-1278 of the 176th FS is at its ANG base at Madison, Wisconsin, August 1974. (SGW)

Above: Not all ANG Daggers had bright colours. **F102A** 56-1361 was operated in a Vietnam period camouflage by the 146th FS Pennsylvania ANG at Pittsburgh, August 1970. (SGW)

Left: The fate of a number of American designs is to be converted to drones and shot down during test work. So it was with the F102. **PQM102B** 56-1254 is seen at Eglin AFB FL, October 1981.

Right: The first of the 'Century Series Fighters' was the **North American F100 Super Sabre**. It was the first operational fighter that was capable of supersonic level flight. **F100D** 56-3011 of the 20th TFW, with the type's 'buzz' number 'FW' on the fuselage, at Finningley, September 1964. (AG)

Right: By the start of the 1970s most of the European Super Sabres had been camouflaged. F100D 56-3213 of 492nd TFS with a two-letter tail code 'LR', or to give it its correct name 'Distinctive Unit Aircraft Identification Markings', was seen at Bentwaters in May 1970.

Above: The French were early users of the Super Sabre. Seen at Sculthorpe, May 1976, is F100D 42249 of EC 2/11. The badge on the fin depicts a black vulture with a white skull in its talons.

Below: Two-seat Super Sabres were designated F100Fs. Showing off its bare metal colours is GT-018, a Royal Danish Air Force example at Bentwaters, May 1970.

Below: By the end of their service life the Danes had toned down the type's markings. TF100F GT-908 of Esk 730 based at Skrydstrup is seen at RAF Valley, August 1981.

Below: With the large cockpit canopy to cover both seats open, this F100F Super Sabre 56-3899 receives maintenance on the ramp at Barnes Field, Westfield, August 1974. This aircraft is operated by 131st FS/104th FG of the Massachusetts ANG. Note that it does not carry ANG markings. (SGW)

Above: This F100D is worthy of note for several reasons. First, its operator is the 3595th Air Demonstration Flight from Nellis AFB, NV, who are of course better known as 'The Thunderbirds'. Second, note the very rare example of non-presentation of the aircraft's serial. It carries the number 'SIX', its place in the team. The proper identity is 55-3715 and it is pictured at Lakenheath, May 1967. (SGW)

Left: Following the fate of many designs the Super Sabre was converted to be a target drone. The red paint on the fin and nose are quick and crude high-visibility devices. On the nose is the conversion number QF098D. This aircraft QF100D 56-2912 is on charge to the 475th TFIS at Tyndall AFB, FL where it was photographed in October 1981.

Below: The **Dassault Mirage 5** was built after a request from the Israeli Air Force for a less sophisticated daylight attack version of the Mirage 111. Before they could be delivered the French government put an embargo on the export and they were absorbed into the French Air Force as the Mirage VF. No. 17 is seen here at Châteaudun undergoing maintenance in June 1977.

Below: The **Convair F106 Delta Dart** was the last of the 'Century Series Fighters'. It was also the last pure interceptor for the USAF, i.e. not being developed into a multi-role aircraft. 57-2495 of the 84th FIS is seen at George AFB, CA, October 1979. The home base was Castle AFB.

Above: The Mirage 5 has proved to be an export success with at least a dozen nations operating the aircraft. Illustrated is **Mirage 5BD** BD03 of 3 Wing, Belgian Air Force. This is a two-seat conversion trainer and is pictured at Finningley, September 1984.

Above: Tyndall AFB in Florida operated Delta Darts for nearly twenty-five years. **F106A** 57-2495 of the 95th FITS is seen departing the ramp in October 1981.

Below: Fresno, California is the home base of the 194th FIS. This ANG unit operated Delta Darts from 1974 to 1984. The tail marking on **F106A** 58-0782 is the bear symbol of the state with the name below. It is at Edwards AFB, October 1979.

Above: The **F106B** was the two-seat type converter. 58-0904 of the 95th FITS, part of the Air Defence Weapons Centre, lands at home base, Tyndall AFB, October 1981.

Above: Conversion to targets was the fate of most Delta Darts. **QF106A** 59-0043 is on charge to the 475th WEG at Tyndall AFB, seen here in April 1994. This airframe also carries extra markings in celebration of the type.

Right: The **Grumman F14 Tomcat** is one of the world's most famous fighter aircraft. With a film career in *Top Gun* and a proven combat record with the US Navy it can be recognised world-wide. 162589 F14A 451/NJ of VF124 shows off its low and slow flying skills at Abbotsford, BC, in August 1986. Note the sparks from the arrester hook as it scrapes the ground.

Left: US Navy squadron VF101 'The Grim Reapers' brought **F14A Tomcat** 162689 101/AD to the EAA Airshow at Oshkosh, WI in August 1986.

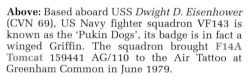

Below: In the mid-1970s Tomcat markings were far more colourful than today. **F14A** 159426 214/AB of VF32 is on the deck of USS *John F. Kennedy* (CVN 67) at Portsmouth, October 1976.

Below: US Navy fighter squadron VF14 'The Top Hatters' claims to be the oldest squadron with a continuous history; it goes back to 1919. With full colour markings **F14A Tomcat** 159593 120/AB is on the deck of USS *John F. Kennedy* at Portsmouth, October 1976.

Above: Based aboard USS *Dwight D. Eisenhower* (CVN 69), US Navy fighter squadron VF143 is known as the 'Pukin Dogs', its badge is in fact a winged Griffin. The squadron brought **F14A Tomcat** 159441 AG/110 to the Air Tattoo at Greenham Common in June 1979.

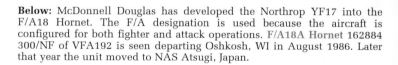

Below: A sight no longer to be seen, a US Navy Tomcat in full colour markings. **F14A** 159449 212/AE of VF142 'Ghostriders' is at Greenham Common, July 1976.

Below: McDonnell Douglas has developed the Northrop YF17 into the F/A18 Hornet. The F/A designation is used because the aircraft is configured for both fighter and attack operations. **F/A18A Hornet** 162884 300/NF of VFA192 is seen departing Oshkosh, WI in August 1986. Later that year the unit moved to NAS Atsugi, Japan.

Left: NAS Patuxent River, MD houses the Naval Air Test Centre. **F/A18A** 161367 152/SD carries high-visibility tail markings to enable it to be tracked during weapon release trials. It is seen at its base, May 1989.

Below: Switzerland is one of the newest operators of the Hornet. **F/A18C** J-5014 of FLst17, Swiss Air Force lands at Fairford, July 1999.

Below: Patuxent River also houses the US Navy Test Pilots School. As expected this unit has a host of different aircraft in many non-standard colours. **F/A18B** 161249 is a two-seat Hornet. It is pictured at its base in May 1989.

Below: Canada was the first export sale for the Hornet. Designated **CF188**, they form the backbone of the Canadian Armed Forces fighter and attack force. CF188 188713 is seen arriving at Hamilton, Ont, June 1990. It is operated by 410 Squadron from Cold Lake Alberta.

Above: Spain has purchased sixty Hornets. Seen here at Boscombe Down, in June 1992, is CE15.9 12-72 of Ala12. This is an **EF18B** two-seat trainer.

Above: Canadian Armed Forces **CF188** 188764 of 439 Squadron is seen in a special camouflage colour scheme at Boscombe Down, June 1992. The tiger stripes had been applied for that year's NATO Tiger Meet.

Below: Finland is in the process of assembling Hornets for delivery to its air force. **F/A18C** HN407 of HaLLv 21 was photographed at its Pirkkala base in June 1998. It is of note that the aircraft has its wings folded. This feature was designed as the US Navy needed this facility for carrier operations. Even though Finland does not operate such ships all aircraft have wing folding capabilities because it would have been more expensive to delete the feature.

Above: Kuwait placed an order for forty Hornets in 1988. The first aircraft was not delivered until January 1992 following the Gulf War that liberated the country from the Iraqi invasion of August 1990. Operated by 9 Squadron from its base at Ahamad Al Jaber is **KA/F18C** 425. It was photographed at Fairford in July 1993.

Right: The best-known Hornet operator is the US Navy Flight Demonstration Team 'The Blue Angels'. They are based at Pensacola NAS and have been seen by millions of people worldwide. They are renowned for their very tight formation keeping. F/A18A 161976 No. 6 is seen at Patuxent River, May 1989.

Below: This F/A18C Hornet of VFA81, 163477 AA/403, shows its markings in black instead of the normal grey on grey. It was photographed at Mildenhall in May 1992.

Below: The McDonnell Douglas F15 Eagle is the US Air Force's premier fighter. It has been so for over twenty years and is likely to be so for some years to come. The first variant was the F15A. 76-0065 of the 405th TFW LA/Luke AFB is seen at its base, October 1979. This airframe crashed on 13 February 1981.

Above: Despite being an advanced aeroplane the Eagle is in service with the part-time ANG. Most of the unit pilots are ex-military and current commercial pilots who have far more flight experience on more types than current regulars. Two Georgia ANG F15As, 75-0043 and 75-0024, of the 128th TFS fly by at the London, Ont Airshow, June 1990.

Above: The F15C is an improved version of the Eagle with provision for conformal fuel tanks. 84-0027 of the 36th FW BT/Bitburg was seen at Mildenhall in May 1992. This aircraft sports two Iraqi kills from the 1991 Gulf War.

Left: Tyndall AFB in Florida is home to a number of Eagle squadrons. F15C 78-0505 is on charge to 2nd FS/325th FW and shows the base TY code. It was photographed in April 1994.

Below: The F15D is the two-seat variant of the F15C. 85-0130 of the 3rd Wing departs from its base at Elmendorf, AK in May 2000 with its afterburners glowing. The yellow fin tip colours indicate it is part of the 54th FS.

Left: The two-seat version of the F15A was the **F15B**. Fifty-seven were ordered. 74-0137 was photographed at LA/Luke AFB, its home with the 405th TFW, in October 1979.

Below: Sukhoi's Su-25 (NATO code-name Frogfoot) is a close air support ground attack jet built to absorb punishment. It has been called the jet successor to the Il2/10 Shturmovik of World War II. 368 OshAP of the Russian Air Force operates **Su-25BM** 09(Red). It was photographed at Damgarten, in the old GDR, in July 1992. The unit has moved back to Russia and is at Budyennovsk. (PJD)

Above: **Su-25K** 9093 is on charge to 322TLT of the Czech Air Force. It was photographed at its base Namest Nad Oslavou, in August 1998. (PJD)

Above: The **F15E Strike Eagle** is a dual-role strike aircraft that retains its air-to-air capability. It can carry a load of over 20,000 lb of weapons. 91-0323/LN of the 48th FW, based at Lakenheath, is seen visiting Tampere, Finland, June 1998.

Above: The special markings on this Czech Air Force **Su-25K** of 30BLP show a frog smashing a tank – a sense of humour from what was once a Warsaw Pact country. The NATO name for the type was Frogfoot and its role was to destroy tanks. It was photographed at Boscombe Down in June 1992.

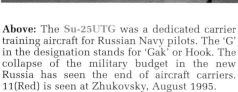

Above: The **Su-25UTG** was a dedicated carrier training aircraft for Russian Navy pilots. The 'G' in the designation stands for 'Gak' or Hook. The collapse of the military budget in the new Russia has seen the end of aircraft carriers. 11(Red) is seen at Zhukovsky, August 1995.

Right: **AMX-T** is the designation of the two-seat trainer. As well as the training airframe there are plans for an electronic warfare variant armed with anti-radar missiles. MM55025 is at the Farnborough Air Show, September 1992.

Above: The **AMX** is a joint venture between Italy and Brazil for a light strike and reconnaissance aircraft. It is powered by a single Rolls-Royce Spey turbofan. MM7131 RS-13/RSV is operated by the Italian Air Force test wing from its base at Pratica di Mare, near Rome. It is pictured at Fairford, July 1995.

Right: The Republic F84F Thunderstreak was a swept-wing variant of the F84 Thunderjet. They were supplied in large numbers to NATO from 1955. This Belgian Air Force example, FU-28, was photographed at Upper Heyford, June 1969. At the end of its service life it was used as a decoy airframe. (SGW)

Below: The Royal Dutch Air Force received 180 examples of the F84F Thunderstreak starting in June 1955. This example is operated by 315 Squadron, based at Eindhoven, which acted as a joint Dutch/Belgian operational conversion unit for the type. P-255 is seen at Chivenor, August 1969. Following Dutch service it was passed to the Greek Air Force.

Above: The Northrop F5 is one of the most widely used lightweight fighters flying today. Named the 'Freedom Fighter', it was conceived as a 'simple' machine when other manufactures were building large complex aeroplanes. Many countries have been upgrading the sophistication levels of their F5s to extend the service life. The Swiss use many of the type. J-3061 F5E is seen at Dübendorf, August 1987.

Left: The Swiss Air Force aerobatic team, '*La Patrouille Suisse*' has flown the F5 since 1994 when the team gave up its Hawker Hunters. F5E J3088 is seen landing at Fairford following a display, July 1995.

Above: The Turkish Air Force operates a mixed bag of F5s, having received them second-hand from a number of countries. The national aerobatic team is the 'Turkish Stars'. NF5A 71-3051 is seen about to take off for a display at Fairford, July 1996.

Above: Showing off its desert camouflage is F5E 1101 of 9 Squadron, Royal Jordanian Air Force. It is pictured on a visit to the UK at Greenham Common, June 1981.

Left: In the early 1960s when Canada chose to licence build the F5 the other aircraft looked at ranged from the Fiat G91 to the General Dynamics F111A. The CF5A or CF116A to give it its service designation suffered from defence cutbacks during the mid-1990s and has been withdrawn from service. **CF5A** 116703 of 419 Squadron shows off a special colour scheme for display purposes at Hamilton, Ont, June 1990. This squadron used the type as a 'lead in' fighter trainer.

Below: Spain has operated the F5 since the 1960s. CASA built them under the designation SF5. Two-seater **SF5B** AE9.–018, 23-26 of Ala 23 was photographed at its base of Talavera la Real in March 1997. This unit provides fast jet training for Hornet pilots. (PJD)

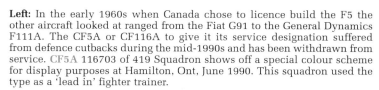

Below: The US Navy has used the F5 as an aggressor training aircraft to give front-line pilots combat flying against a dissimilar type of aircraft to their own. **F5E** 162307 10/S of VF43 'Challengers' is at Tyndall, FL, April 1994.

Below: Operating the same type of aggressor role for the USAF in Europe was the 527th TFTAS at RAF Alconbury. **F5E** 74-1559 was photographed at its base in October 1978. Each of the unit's aircraft had a different type of colour scheme to reflect the operating environment.

Left: Showing off a colour scheme that would have been common a decade earlier is **F5B** 73-1602 of the 405th TTW at Williams AFB, AZ, photographed in October 1979. The HQ of the unit was at nearby Luke AFB but the F5s operated from Williams because of the commonality with the based T38 Talons.

Above: Holland chose the F5 in 1966 to replace its F84Fs. The aircraft were built in Canada by Canadair and are designated **NF5A** or B. K3026 NF5A of 314 Squadron was photographed at Greenham Common in July 1983. The aircraft is in special airshow markings with the national colours displayed.

Left: The Royal Norwegian Air Force ordered F5s in 1964 to augment its expensive F104 Starfighters; they are still in service. **F5B** 136 of 338 Squadron is seen at Valley, August 1981.

Right: 336 Squadron of the Royal Norwegian Air Force is the last unit with the type. **F5A** 208 is in special colours for the NATO Tiger Meet at Fairford, July 1995.

Below: Illustrated is **MiG-21PFM** 4803 of the Romanian Air Force. It is operated by the 86th *Regiment de Vinatoare*. It was photographed at Feteçti in May 1999. (PJD)

Below: The Russian MiG-21 has been one of the widest used supersonic fighters. The early Fishbed, to use the NATO code-name, was a basic lightweight fighter with a low level of sophistication but a high performance. As the design was developed it grew into a heavier and increasingly better-equipped aircraft. In August 1995, 62(Green) a two-seat variant **MiG-21UM** (NATO code-name Mongol) was photographed at the Russian test centre at Zhukovsky.

Above: A major update of Romania's MiG-21s is taking place in conjunction with the Israeli company ELBIT Defence Systems. They are upgrading the fighters systems; such modified aircraft have the new name Lancer. **MiG-21UM Lancer B** 9511 of SMAS was photographed at Bacau in May 1999. (PJD)

Below: The **MiG-21MF (Fishbed – J)** is a second-generation aeroplane with a more powerful radar and powerplant. 7701 of 4 ZSL of the Czech Air Force shows off a very distinctive air superiority colour scheme. It was photographed at Hradec Králové in August 1998. (SGW)

Above: The third generation variant from MiG was the **MiG-21bis**. One of the many countries to operate them was Finland. MG138 of HavLLa 31, the based unit, was photographed at Rissala in June 1998. Nearly fifty nations have operated versions of the MiG-21.

Above: Polish Naval Aviation **MiG-21UM** 9232 of 1 DLMW was seen taking off from its base at Gdynia Babie Doly in April 1998. (PJD)

Left: Showing off two different colour schemes is **MiG-21UM** 3756 of the Czech Air Force Test Centre. It shows a cartoon-like image on the aircraft. It is pictured at Fairford, July 1996.

Below: Czech Air Force **MiG-21MF** 7711 is seen at Fairford. The basic camouflage has been over-painted with high-visibility markings in the national colours.

Above: The **Dassault Mirage F1** was the company's successor to the very popular Mirage 111 family of jets. As well as France it has been sold to ten other air arms. Seen at Leuchars, in September 1974, was No. 24 30-FB of Esc 30 based at Reims.

Below: The Spanish Air Force – *Ejercito del Aire* bought seventy-three Mirage F1s in five batches between March 1973 and March 1983. Ten more airframes were purchased from the Qatari Air Force. **Mirage F1EE** C.14-54 is operated by Ala14 and based at Los Llanos. It was seen visiting Fairford in July 1997.

Above: Ecuador purchased sixteen single-seat and two two-seat Mirage F1s. These aircraft saw action when they fought skirmishes with the Peruvian Air Force over a long-running border dispute. **Mirage F1JA** FAE808 is at Latacunga AFB, September 1997.

Above: Mirage F1s were ordered by Jordan to replace its Lockheed F104 Starfighters. **Mirage F1EJ** 107 is in desert colours at Fairford, and was photographed in July 1987. It is operated by No. 1 Squadron based at Mowafaq al Salti air base.

Below: The two-seat trainer version of the Fiat G91 was the **G91T**. Seen at Cottesmore, in July 1989, was MM54408 of 60 *Brigata* based at Armendola. This is the advanced training wing of the Italian Air Force.

Above: In 1954 NATO requested a lightweight fighter and ground attack aircraft. The selected design was the Fiat G91. As well as Italy the air forces of West Germany and Portugal operated them, and it was even evaluated by the US Army. **Fiat G91R** 31+88 of Lkg 41 is seen at Chivenor, August 1969.

Above: To celebrate 75,000 hours of flying its Fiat G91 fleet the Portuguese Air Force applied special markings to this aeroplane. **Fiat G91R** 5445 of Esq 301 is adorned with the badges of all the units operating the type as well as all the pilots' names. It is at Fairford, July 1993.

Right: The tiger colours of this Portuguese Air Force **Fiat G91R** 5452 of Esq 301 must be among the most spectacular that have been applied to any aircraft for the NATO Tiger Meet. It was photographed at Fairford in July 1991.

Above: The **Su-27** featured is seen on final approach to land Fairford, July 1997.

Above: Sukhoi's 'Flanker' stable of long-range fighters has astonished the west with its performances both with range and manoeuvrability. The first in line is the **Su-27**. Ukrainian Air Force example 57 of 62/83 IAP was photographed at Fairford in July 1996.

Below: Designed for use on the planned aircraft carriers, the **Su-33 (Su-27K)** has folding wings and tail. It is basically a naval version of the air force fighter. 109 (Flanker D) is seen at Zhukovsky, August 1995.

Above: The **Su-30** is a two-seat long-range interceptor with the facility for air-to-ground weapons. 52 (Blue) is a Russian example operated by 148th TsBPlPels (Flight Personnel Combat Training & Conversion Unit) based at Savostleyka. It is seen landing at Fairford, July 1997.

Above: The **Su-35 (Su-27M)** was developed as a multi-role interceptor and ground attack aircraft. The plan was for it to replace a number of single role types. 703 is seen at Zhukovsky, August 1995.

Below: This plan view of a **Su-27IB** shows what a different aircraft it is to the basic Su-27. It has two seats in a side-by-side configuration and is the prototype for a long-range attack aircraft. 42 is seen at Zhukovsky, August 1995.

Below: A planned replacement for the Sukhoi Su-24 'Fencer' is the Su-34. The aircraft is much larger than the basic Su-27, the main undercarriage is a double-wheel unit, access is via a ladder under the nose and it even has a toilet. 45 is a prototype for the design with the designation **Su-34FN**. It has been configured for attacks on shipping and is seen at Zhukovsky, August 1995.

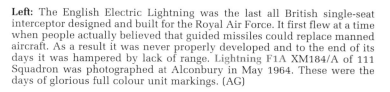

Left: The English Electric Lightning was the last all British single-seat interceptor designed and built for the Royal Air Force. It first flew at a time when people actually believed that guided missiles could replace manned aircraft. As a result it was never properly developed and to the end of its days it was hampered by lack of range. Lightning F1A XM184/A of 111 Squadron was photographed at Alconbury in May 1964. These were the days of glorious full colour unit markings. (AG)

Below: The Lightning F1A was the second version to enter service and it had in-flight refuelling capability. XM182 was photographed on a wet day at Upper Heyford in June 1971, in the markings of 65 Squadron. This unit was a 'shadow' squadron and part of 226 OCU, the training unit.

Above: Each of the early Lightning bases had their own Target Facilities Flight. The task of these units was to provide whole aircraft targets for the based squadrons, the usual fleet was three aircraft. Lightning F1A XM139 is in the markings of Wattisham TFF and is seen landing at Bentwaters, May 1972.

Above: The third variant was the F2 Lightning. These were issued to 19 and 92 Squadrons who spent the larger part of their lives as interceptors for RAF Germany. Most of the F2s were converted to F2A standard and to many this version was the best to fly. In April 1976 XN727, a Lightning F2A of W/92 Squadron, was at Valley for missile practice camp.

Left: The F3 was the fourth variant of single-seater and could be quickly spotted by the clipped tail top. Lightning F3 XR716 of 226 OCU is at Chivenor, August 1970.

Below: As well as the previously illustrated 65 Squadron, 226 OCU added another unit. This was simply called 2T and did not have a squadron number plate. Lightning F3 XP696 showed its markings off at Leuchars, September 1974.

Below: The Lightning Training Flight (LTF) was formed in October 1975; the OCU had disbanded in September of the previous year when the run down of the type was in sight. The Lightning proved too difficult to get rid of so the new unit was formed to train more pilots. Lightning F3 XP749 A/LTF is at the unit base of Binbrook, August 1978. Camouflage had descended on the type by this time.

Below: Lightning F3 XR719 of D/56 Squadron has what must be the finest colour scheme to adorn any unit's aircraft. It was photographed at Lakenheath in May 1965. Following this scheme the Air Council ordered that markings be subdued. (AG)

Right: A wonderful line up of Lightning F3s was seen at Wattisham in May 1968. At the end of the line is XP756 of K/29 Squadron, which was based at this location. (AG)

Above: Near the end of the Lightning's service life a number of aircraft had their camouflage replaced with air defence grey. Lightning F3 XP749 of BK/11 Squadron is seen at Yeovilton, August 1984.

Above: When the first pilots converted to the Lightning they did so without the aid of a two-seat trainer. In the early days of operations only experienced crews got to fly the type not pilots straight from training – this policy was later changed. The trainer for the F1/F2 was the T4 and featured side-by-side seating. XM995 of T/92 Squadron was photographed landing at Valley, August 1976.

Left: This picture of T4 XM995 of T/92 Squadron shows the different nose shape of the two-seater. It was photographed at Wildenrath in June 1978.

Below: To train F3/F6 pilots the two-seater used was the T5; this had the clipped fin top of these two variants. XS419 of T/23 Squadron is at the unit's base Leuchars, September 1975.

Below: The first unit to get the definitive Lightning was 5 Squadron at Binbrook. This was the F6 and had the larger ventral fuel tank. XR772, E/5 Squadron is seen departing its base, May 1972.

Above: To extend the range for ferry flights Lightnings could carry over-wing tanks. XP769 of J/11 Squadron is seen departing Binbrook, May 1972.

Below: 'The Firebirds', 56 Squadron were based at Akrotiri in Cyprus from 1967 to 1975. During this time they exchanged their F3s for F6s. XS897 Lightning F6, S/56 Squadron, is seen at Lakenheath following their return to the UK (August 1975). Their new base was Wattisham.

Above: NATO gave the reporting name Fulcrum to the MiG-29. This aircraft is a relatively small interceptor with a very high performance from its two RD33 bypass turbofans. The output is 18,300 lb st (with afterburner/reheat). It was first seen in the west during a 1988 visit to Farnborough. However its secrets were laid bare when the East German air force was integrated into the *Luftwaffe* following the country's reunification. 29+14 of JG73 is seen at Mildenhall, May 1996.

Below: January 1993 saw the peaceful separation of the Czech and Slovak republics. The two nations split the stock of MiG-29s equally between themselves. 6829 of 1SLP Slovak Air Force is at Fairford, July 1996.

Above: MiG-29 3911 of 11SLP was photographed before the split at Boscombe Down in June 1992 in the colours of the Czechoslovakian Air Force.

Above: Seen on the ramp at Constanta/Mikhail Kogalniceanu, the base of the 57th Regiment Romanian Air Force is MiG-29 70(Red). It was photographed in May 1999. (PJD)

Below: MiG-29 103 is in the colours of the 'Ukrainian Falcons' aerobatic team. It is seen at Fairford, July 1997.

Above: Arriving back from a display, with its braking parachute still attached, is Russian MiG-29UB 86(Blue). It was photographed at Zhukovsky in August 1995.

Below: Now a member of NATO, Hungary has left what was the 'Warsaw Pact' group as that alliance has now collapsed. Seen landing at Fairford in July 1998 was MiG-29UB 25(Red) of the 59th Tactical Fighter Regiment. Note the periscope above the rear seat cockpit.

Right: Seen on the ramp at its home base of Minsk-Mazowiecki is Polish Air Force **MiG-29** 111(Red) of 1 PLM. It was photographed in April 1998. (PJD)

Below: The **MiG-29K** is the variant designed for use on the Russian Navy aircraft carriers. 312(Blue) is at Zhukovsky, August 1995, showing its folding wings.

Below: The SEPECAT Jaguar is a joint venture between the British and French aircraft industries to build a low-level attack aeroplane. Seen at Binbrook (August 1978) is **Jaguar GR1** XX758 of 18/226 OCU, the Royal Air Force conversion unit for the type.

Above: No. II(AC) Army Co-operation Squadron, RAF, has a history dating back to 1912. It usually portrays its squadron number in Roman numerals rather than as No. 2. Its role is that of tactical reconnaissance. **Jaguar GR1** XZ103 of II/2 Squadron is at Wildenrath, June 1978. The Tornado has replaced the type with this squadron.

Below: **Jaguar GR1A** XX725 of GU/54 Squadron, RAF is at Scampton, July 1991. It is in desert camouflage and shows the missions flown in the Gulf War earlier that year. Note that for self-protection the Jaguar can carry air-to-air missiles above the wings.

Above: Following an uprating to its Adour engines and various upgrades to the electronics and navigation systems the Jaguar was redesignated **GR1A**. XZ396 of EM/6 Squadron, RAF, was photographed at Fairford in July 1999, in the current grey colour scheme.

Below: Seen landing at Abingdon (September 1990) is **Jaguar GR1A** XZ399 of 03/226 OCU. The radar warning receiver on the fin has a tartan band on it to indicate its then Scottish base at Lossiemouth. On the intake is the unit badge of the 'Torch and Quiver'.

Below: The two-seat trainer Jaguar is the **T2**. Seen in 'raspberry ripple' colours is XX830 of the Empire Test Pilots School. It was seen departing Fairford in July 1989.

Above: Following the disbandment of 16 Squadron as a Tornado unit its numberplate was transferred to the Jaguar OCU. **Jaguar GR1A** XX116 of 16(R) Squadron was photographed at Fairford in July 1995. The black colour is for appearances at airshows. The 'saint' motif on the fin dates from the time it was formed at St Omer, France, in 1915.

Below: The second nation in the Jaguar design is France. They designated the aircraft as either a Jaguar A (single-seat) or Jaguar E (two-seat). The French aircraft have not been as highly upgraded as the RAF ones and lack such features as a laser range finder in the nose. Seen at Fassberg, West Germany, is A147 **Jaguar A** 11-EF of EC1/11.

Above: French Air Force **Jaguar E** E30 7-PK of EC.02.007 was photographed at Tampere, in Finland June 1998. The aircraft had travelled from its base at St Dizier to take part in an airshow.

Below: The fighter version of the Panavia Tornado was a British only requirement between the three nations that built the aeroplane (Italy and Germany were the other two), however the Italian Air Force has since leased a number of RAF aircraft. The basic difference between the bomber and fighter versions is that the latter has a longer fuselage and an air defence radar. **Tornado F2** ZD932 of AM/229 OCU is at RAF Conningsby, June 1985. The F2 was an interim version before the main production batch of F3s.

Above: With the arrival of the **Tornado F3 ADV** – Air Defence Variant – the training unit, 229 OCU got a shadow squadron numberplate. This was 65 Squadron; it once had the same role for Lightnings. ZE339 of AO/229, OCU 65 Squadron, is seen at North Weald, May 1989. Note the new markings on the nose but the retention of the OCU colours of a 'Torch and Sword' on the fin.

Left: In July 1992 229 OCU was renumbered as 56(R) Squadron. The unit was also tasked with providing an example for airshows. **Tornado F3** ZE839 of AR/56(R) Squadron is at Mildenhall, May 1993. It shows off the sort of markings the squadron had been famous for in the past. The badge is a Phoenix.

Below: Toned down markings are seen in this more recent picture of a 56 Squadron **Tornado F3**. ZE292 AZ/ was photographed landing at Fairford in July 1999, following a display.

Right: The Lockheed F104 Starfighter was once called the 'missile with a man in it'. Its pencil-slim shaped fuselage and thin sharp wings were years ahead of its rivals in style. Designed for the USAF it only served them briefly but formed the cold war backbone of NATO and was operated by fourteen air arms. Seen here in toned down markings is **F104S-ASA** CMX-611 RS-06 of the Italian Air Force RSV (*Reparto Sperimentale di Volo*). This is a test wing; the F104S-ASA is one with new avionics as well as modifications to other systems. It is seen landing at Fairford, July 1998.

Left: 23 Squadron was one of the units that fell foul of the 'peace dividend' at the end of the cold war. **Tornado F3** ZE809 EZ/ is in special markings to celebrate the seventy-fifth anniversary of the unit. It is pictured at Finningley, September 1990.

Below: One of the two **Tornado F3** units based at Leeming, 25 Squadron had not operated aircraft for some time having been a Bloodhound missile unit prior to conversion. ZE167 is seen at Duxford in special markings, July 1991.

Below: A small unit but a vital one. The **F3** OEU (Operational Evaluation Unit) is tasked with updating the 'handbook' on the type by use of new tactics and operational trials. ZE729 is seen at the unit's base, Conningsby, June 1989.

Above: Seen here in 'normal' Italian Air Force colours with full size codes is MM6728 53-14 of 21 *Gruppo*. It was attending the Tiger Meet at Upper Heyford in June 1971. This is an **F104S** built in Italy by Aeritalia and is an upgrade of the F104G.

Below: Showing off a very special colour scheme is **F104S-ASA** MM6827 of the Italian Air Force RSV. The markings are to celebrate the fiftieth anniversary of the unit. It was seen at Fairford, July 1999. (SGW)

Below: The Netherlands was one of the NATO countries that bought the Lockheed Starfighter in what was referred to as 'the sale of the century'. Fokker built most of these aircraft in Holland. **F104G** D-8311 of 323 Squadron is seen at Leuchars, September 1974. This was an all-weather interceptor unit based at Leeuwarden; the squadron flew the type from 1964 to 1980.

Below: Seen making a fast pass at Leuchars is Royal Dutch Air Force **F104G** D6654 of 323 Squadron. The type's distinctive shape was captured in this photograph taken in September 1973.

Above: The Turkish Air Force has over the years acquired a vast number of second-hand Starfighters from other NATO nations. In July 1993, 5704 8-704 of 181 *Filo* was photographed at Fairford. This is a two-seat **TF104G**.

Below: The 58th TTW operated both single- and two-seat Starfighters. 13080 is a **TF104G** two-seat conversion trainer. It is at Luke AFB, October 1979.

Below: The F104 had a short life with the USAF; most were gone by the mid-1960s with the ANG hanging on for another ten years. The **F104G** illustrated is 67-14890 of the 58th TTW. This training unit is operated by the *Luftwaffe* to train its pilots in the Arizona sunshine, hence the American markings. It was photographed at its base, Luke AFB, in October 1979.

Below: Norway purchased a number of Canadair-built Starfighters following the Canadian defence cuts of the early 1970s. Seen at Upper Heyford in July 1976 is **CF104** 104755 of 331 Skv who were based at Bodø. The unit flew this type between 1963 and 1981.

Below: Canadian Armed Forces (CAF) Starfighter **CF104** 104865 has a Vicon reconnaissance pod fitted to the underside of the fuselage. This could house up to four 70 mm Vinten cameras. It is seen on a very wet June day in 1971 at Upper Heyford in the early silver colour scheme.

Below: CAF **CF104** 104756 was painted up for its visit to the NATO Tiger Meet at Upper Heyford in July 1976. 439 Squadron, based at Barden-Sollingen in West Germany, operates it.

Above: Seen at Wildenrath in June 1978 is Belgian Air Force **F104G** FX76 of 10 Wing based at Kleine Brogel. This air arm's aircraft were assembled by SABCA. Like most other NATO countries the Starfighter was replaced by the F16.

Right: West Germany was the largest user of the Starfighter, the *Luftwaffe* having 766 and the *Marineflieger* 151, a total of 917. The aircraft in German service were tarred with having a poor safety record and called the 'widow maker'. Over 250 were lost. In percentage terms this was a lower rate than some other NATO forces. 27+34, a two-seat **TF104G** of JBG 33, was photographed at Lakenheath in August 1975.

Above: Single-seat **F104G** 21+98 of JBG 33 is at Wildenrath, June 1978. It is taking part in a NATO Tactical Weapons Meet and has had the extra code letter 'E' applied to the fin. *Luftwaffe* aircraft do not usually carry such codes.

Below: This Danish Air Force **F104G** R-647 is seen in the delivery anti-corrosion grey colour scheme. Most of the Danish aircraft were Canadian-built. It is seen at Coltishall, September 1968. (SGW)

Above: This Messerschmitt-built **F104G** is operated by the German Navy and has the name 'Marine' on the rear fuselage. It is VB+229 of MFG 2 based at Eggebeck. Note the early use of mixed alpha/numeric code. It was photographed at Brawdy in August 1968.

Above: Most of the careers of Denmark's Starfighters were spent in this all-over dark green scheme. **F104G** R-704 of Aalborg-based Esk 726 is at Binbrook, September 1977.

Below: The **Vought F8 Crusader** was known in US Navy service as 'the last of the gunfighters'. A single-seat and -engined (Pratt & Whitney J57) fighter it had a performance of over 1000 mph. The last users of the type were the French Navy who retired them late in 1999. F8E No. 40 of 12F is seen at Yeovilton, July 1972.

Below: The last regular US Navy use of the Crusader was as a photo reconnaissance aircraft. **RF8G** 144607 602/AB was operated by VFP63 which was the last dedicated PR unit in the navy flying the last dedicated PR aeroplane. The unit operated the type for twenty-one years until 1982. It was photographed onboard USS *John F. Kennedy* in October 1976. Note the square camera ports under the stars and bars national markings.

Left: F8K 145580 of the US Navy Test Pilots School was photographed at Patuxent River in June 1972. The 'K' model was a remanufactured F8C with various upgrades. (SGW)

Below: The Hawker Hunter has been one of the great success stories for the British aviation industry. First flown in July 1951 it is still in limited service with a number of air forces world-wide. Illustrated is Hunter F6 XJ639 of 31/234 Squadron, the 'shadow' for the TWU – Tactical Weapons Unit. It was photographed at Binbrook in July 1975. The F6 entered squadron service during 1956 and had a more powerful Rolls-Royce Avon engine together with improved flying controls.

Above: Seen landing at Dübendorf (August 1987) is Hunter F58 J-4053 of the Swiss Air Force. This air arm selected the type following a multi-type competition and went on to operate nearly 150. They were replaced by the F5 during the 1990s. The F58 was an export F6.

Above: The Chilean Air Force operated Hunter Mk71 and Mk72s, single- and two-seaters respectively. Hunter FGA71 J-728 was seen at Chester in June 1971, prior to delivery. This aircraft is an ex-RAF F6 (XE644).

Above: The Royal Jordanian Air Force operated Hunters until 1975 when the current stock was presented to the Sultan of Oman. Seen prior to delivery at Chester in June 1971, is Hunter Mk73 842. This was a re-conditioned ex-RAF F6.

Above: The ultimate Hunter was the FGA9, a fighter ground-attack variant built from F6s; none were new-built. XE601 is seen at Finningley in September 1989 and is operated by the A&AEE at Boscombe Down. The type serves to this day.

Above: Hunter FGA9 XK137 42/ of 45 Squadron is seen at Greenham Common in July 1976. This squadron was reformed in 1972, along with No. 58, at Wittering to provide the RAF with an increased ground-attack capacity but more importantly to develop a pool of pilots versed in this demanding role.

Right: WW598, a Hunter F6 of the Royal Aircraft Establishment was photographed at Llanbedr in July 1969. This modified aircraft features an extended nose. Note the Welsh Dragon on the base of the nose.

Below: The two-seat **Hunter T7** trainer did not enter service until 1958. This had required the first generation of Hunter pilots to convert to type without the aid of a dedicated trainer. XL591 of 82/4 FTS was photographed at its base, Valley, in August 1976 in the then current training colour scheme.

Above: **Hunter T7** XL573 is seen at Finningley, September 1989. 12 Squadron, at the time a Buccaneer unit, operates this aircraft. The reason for the Hunter's presence was that there were no two-stick Buccaneers so each squadron had a Hunter converted to Buccaneer-style instruments in the left-hand seat. This eased the conversion to type process. Another use was to give pilots flight experience whilst the squadron's own aircraft were grounded.

Above: The BAe Harrier serving today with the RAF can trace its roots from the Hawker P1127 VTOL research aircraft. The success of the type was to have engine nozzles that rotated from down for take-off to back for level flight. When the P1127 first flew in 1960 most other VTOL projects had two sets of engines, one for lift and the other for wing borne flight. This was impractical due to carrying the weight of engines not used in normal flight. The P1127 led to the Kestrel and then to the Harrier. **Harrier GR1** XV741 of A/3 Squadron is seen at Valley, August 1973. This unit was part of 2nd TAF based in Germany.

Above: **Hunter T7** XL617 of 95/229 OCU is seen at its Chivenor base, August 1969. This unit was tasked with converting pilots to Hunters and then teaching them to 'fight' the aircraft. Following the move to Brawdy the unit was re-named Tactical Weapons Unit.

Above: The Royal Navy used Hunters as weapons trainers. The GA11 was a Naval F4; it was not however used on aircraft carriers as it was not equipped with an arrester hook. **Hunter GA11** WV256 862/VL of FRADU (Fleet Requirements & Aircraft Direction Unit) is at its Yeovilton base, July 1994.

Above: XL603, photographed at Fairford in July 1985, is a **Hunter T8M** 720/ of 899 Squadron. The T8 is the Fleet Air Arm variant of the T7 trainer. This special version features an extended nose with radar to train Sea Harrier pilots. 899 Squadron is the Royal Navy training unit for the Sea Harrier.

Below: The next squadron variant of the Harrier GR1 was the **GR3**. XZ129 3C of 233 OCU is seen in the hover at Fairford, July 1989. This version can be recognised by the nose-mounted laser range finder and the radar warning receiver on the leading edge of the fin.

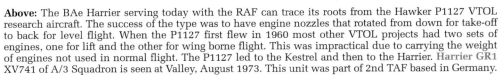

Above: No. 1 Squadron of the RAF can claim to be the oldest military flying unit in the world. It can trace its history to an 1878 balloon unit. It was fitting that it was the first unit in the world to operate a VTOL aircraft. XZ133, a **Harrier GR3** 10 of No. 1 Squadron, is at Lee-on-Solent, July 1987. The white paint over the basic green colour is due to the fact the unit deploys to Norway for winter exercises and this has proved to be an effective camouflage.

Below: No. 1 Squadron currently operates the Harrier GR7. ZG471 61 of 1 Squadron was photographed at Tampere, Finland in June 1998 attending an airshow. The GR7 is a new generation aircraft; it was developed with McDonnell Douglas and is a world away from the P1127.

Above: This two-seater is the second variant of the Harrier trainer and is designated T4. ZD990 Q of 20 Squadron is at Cottesmore, July 1993.

Below: The T10 Harrier is a combat-capable trainer based on the new generation airframe. ZH654 of the A&AEE is at Fairford, July 1995.

Below: Like a number of types the first Harrier pilots converted, in 1969, without the aid of a two-seater. The T2 was soon forthcoming the following year. XW926 M of 3 Squadron is at Valley in August 1973. It shows the extended nose and tall tail of the trainer.

Below: In February 1963 P1127 XP831 landed on HMS *Ark Royal* and thus started a move to see the type in service with the Fleet Air Arm. Sea Harrier FRS1 XZ453 105 of 899 Squadron is at Greenham Common in June 1981. The main difference between RAF and RN aircraft was the role. The navy designation Fighter/Reconnaisance/Strike tells it all. For the first part it is equipped with a Ferranti Blue Fox air defence radar. RAF Harriers are not equipped with this.

Above: Sea Harrier FRS1 XZ458 124/H of 800 Squadron at Mildenhall in May 1981. This unit was based onboard HMS *Hermes*; hence the 'H' code. These colourful markings were removed within twelve months. The reason for this was the Falklands War with Argentina, a conflict in which the type excelled, not losing a single airframe to enemy aircraft.

Right: Showing its post-Falklands markings is Sea Harrier FRS1 ZD610 711 of 899 Squadron, the type's training unit. It is at Hatfield, July 1987.

Right: The mid-life upgrade of the Sea Harrier resulted in the **F/A2**, the new style designation for its role as a fighter/attack aircraft. It features a new radar and many other updates. ZA176 716 of 899 Squadron is at Yeovilton, July 1994. F/A2s are either converted FRS1s as in this case or newly-built aircraft.

Above: Showing off a very distinctive colour scheme is Spanish **TAV8S** VAE1-2 of Esc 008. Seen at Fairford, this two-seater is based at Cádiz.

Below: In Spanish service the Harrier II is designated **EAV 8B**. VA2-5 01/9055 of Esc 009 was seen on a visit to the Royal Navy Harrier base, Yeovilton, in July 1994.

Above: The responsibility of training US Marine Corps Harrier pilots lies with Cherry Point-based VMAT 203 'Hawks'. **TAV8B** 163196 06/KD is seen at Tyndall AFB, April 1994.

Above: The US Marine Corps began Harrier operations in 1971 and has been a very important user of the type. **AV8A** 158969 CG/04 of VMA231 'Aces' is seen onboard USS *Iwo Jima*, October 1980.

Below: Spain began naval Harrier operations in 1976 with the **AV8A(S)**; the type has been named 'Matador'. They were acquired via the USA as Britain had an arms embargo with the Spanish government of General Franco at the time. VA1-3 of Esc 008 is seen at Fairford, July 1994.

Left: In 1989, following a long battle with the government, the Italian Navy was granted permission to operate fixed-wing aircraft. They fly from the 'ski jump'-equipped 13,370-ton aircraft carrier *Giuseppe Garibaldi*. **TAV8B** Harrier MM55032 1-01 is seen at Yeovilton, July 1994.

Below: Based at Fresno the 194th FIS of the California ANG operated **F4D** Phantoms from 1983, when they replaced F106s, until 1989 when they were supplanted by F16s. 65-0763 was photographed arriving back at its base in August 1986 in a smart grey scheme.

Above: It would not be an overstatement to call the **McDonnell F4 Phantom II** the most important western military aircraft of the post-war period. It has served twelve nations, of whom ten still operate it. Seen on the ramp at Luke AFB, AZ, in October 1979 is **F4C** 64-0660 of the based 58th TTW. The green fin top marks it to be of the 310th TFTS, one of three squadrons within the wing. Note the three MiG kills on the splitter plate.

Left: The F4D was the first variant of the Phantom designed to USAF specification; the F4C was almost a basic US Navy F4B. It was the avionics suite that had the major changes. **F4D** 65-0735/LN was seen at Lakenheath in August 1975 and is operated by the based 48th TFW and on charge to the 494th TFS.

Above: The F4E was the most produced variant of the Phantom. The major changes included the fitting of a gun under the nose and wing slats for extra dogfighting capability. **F4E** 66-0382 of the 57th FIS is at Greenham Common, July 1983. This unit was based at Keflavik in Iceland and made many intercepts of Russian patrol aircraft.

Above: The 'HF' tail codes on this line of **F4E**s indicate that they belong to the 113th TFS of the Indiana ANG, based at Hulman Field, Terre Haute. 68-0463 heads the line on the ramp at Reno Cannon, NV, September 1988.

Below: Wild Weasel was the name given to the very dangerous role of hunting surface-to-air missile sites and their radars. The designation F4G was used for this variant (it had been previously been used by the US Navy for a minor version that was no longer in service). The F4Gs were rebuilt F4Es and carried the latest radar receivers and anti-radiation missiles to deal with them. **F4G** 69-0272/WW of the 35th TFW based at George AFB, CA is at London, Ont, June 1990.

Above: The photo reconnaissance Phantom, the RF4C, was based on the F4C airframe with the provision for weapons delivery removed. A new camera nose was the main external difference. RF4C 64-1073 of the 10th TRW based at Alconbury is seen at Lakenheath, May 1967, in the grey/white markings with full colour national insignia. Note it also carries the 'FJ' buzz code of the type. (SGW)

Below: Within a few years the **RF4Cs** had adopted the standard camouflage colours of brown and green. 67-0469/AR is at Wildenrath, June 1978. It is operated by 1st TRS/10th TRW, based at Alconbury.

Above: Seen on the ramp at its base of Reno Cannon in September 1988 is **RF4C** 64-1005 of the 192nd TRS Nevada ANG. The name on the fin top is 'High Rollers'; this relates to the legal gambling in the state.

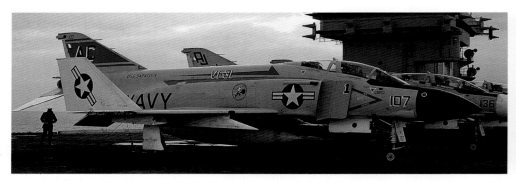

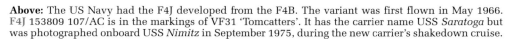

Above: The US Navy had the F4J developed from the F4B. The variant was first flown in May 1966. **F4J** 153809 107/AC is in the markings of VF31 'Tomcatters'. It has the carrier name USS *Saratoga* but was photographed onboard USS *Nimitz* in September 1975, during the new carrier's shakedown cruise.

Above: 65-0713 was the third built **YF4E** and was converted from an F4D. It is seen on charge of the AFFTC at Edwards AFB, CA, October 1979.

Above: In September 1975 **F4J** 153893 135/AJ of US Marine Corps fighter squadron VMFA 333 'Shamrocks' was photographed onboard USS *Nimitz* (CVN 68). Shore-based at Beaufort SC, this unit scored the only USMC air-to-air kill in the Vietnam War when one of its Phantoms destroyed a MiG-21.

Above: The sad fate of many front-line fighters was to be converted into target drones. **QRF4C** 65-0944 of the 475th WEG (82nd ATRS) is at its base of Tyndall, FL, April 1994.

Below: US Navy unit VF171'Aces' was the Atlantic Fleet F4 Fleet Replacement Squadron. **F4J** 155748 205/AD is at Harlingen, TX, October 1979.

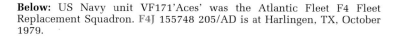

Above: The US Navy converted F4Bs into **QF4B** drones whilst the type was still in front-line service. 149428 is operated by the Pacific Missile Test Centre, Point Magu, CA where it was photographed in October 1976 in this high-visibility dayglo-orange colour. (SGW)

Below: Turkey has been and still is a major **Phantom** operator, and has flown both new and ex-USAF aircraft. 68-0342/7-342 of 7AJU, based at Erhac, is at Boscombe Down, June 1992.

Above: **F4C** C12.40 of Ala 12 (12 Wing) Spanish Air Force was photographed landing at Greenham Common in June 1979. This air arm formed its first Phantom unit in March 1971 with a delivery of refurbished USAF aircraft.

Below: Greece operates both new and ex-USAF F4E and RF4E Phantoms. Seen at Fairford is **RF4E** 7529 of 348 Mira, July 1998.

Below: Germany has been a major user of the Phantom. **RF4E** 35+81 of AKG 51 was photographed at Binbrook in July 1975.

Above: The F4F Phantom was a special German variant. It was in essence a simplified and lighter F4E with many parts built in Germany and shipped to St Louis for final assembly. 37+86, an **F4F** of JG 71 'Richthofen', based at Wittmundhafen was photographed at Binbrook in September 1977.

Below: Britain's Royal Navy became the first export customer of the Phantom when an order was placed in 1964 for a Rolls-Royce Spey engined variant. XT869, a **Phantom FG1** (F4K) 154/VL of 767 Squadron, is at Yeovilton, July 1972. This squadron was the conversion unit for all RN pilots and the first RAF ones.

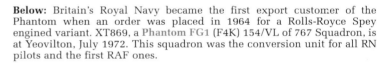

Right: When 767 Squadron disbanded in August 1972 its training role was taken up the following month with the formation of the Phantom Post Operational Conversion Unit at Leuchars. This was a unique unit in that an RAF unit trained Navy crews in RAF aircraft painted in a Navy colour scheme. **Phantom FG1** XT866/W is at its base, September 1977.

Below: The only front-line Royal Navy unit to operate the Phantom was 892 Squadron; the sole carrier used was HMS *Ark Royal*. **Phantom FG1** XV587 010/R of this unit was photographed departing its shore base of RAF Leuchars, in September 1976, with afterburners glowing. The Royal Navy flag on the fuselage has the dates 876–1976 on either side of it. This was a friendly dig at the Americans who were celebrating their bicentennial in that year. It was a boast from the senior service of its roots.

Above: In 1965 the RAF ordered Phantoms designated F4Ms. The first squadron to operate the type was No. 43 at Leuchars. However they formed using **FG1**s that were not needed by the Royal Navy. XV576/D was photographed at its base in September 1976.

Above: The last Phantom to be operated by the UK armed forces was **FG1** XT597. The A&AEE used it as a high-speed chase aircraft. It carries the 'raspberry ripple' colours of many of that unit's trial aircraft. It was photographed at its Boscombe Down base in June 1992.

Below: In RAF service the F4M was designated **FGR2** (Fighter/Ground Attack/Reconnaissance). 41 Squadron specialised in the latter task. They first flew Phantoms in April 1972 but kept them for only five years before becoming a Jaguar unit. XV418 is seen at Leuchars, September 1974.

Above: Sixty years after Alcock and Brown made the first flight across the Atlantic Ocean in a Vickers Vimy another Alcock and Brown flew it in a Phantom, a little more quickly! This 228 OCU **FGR2**, XV424, is in the special colours to commemorate this historic event. It is seen at Abingdon, September 1979.

Above: The second Leuchars-based squadron was 111. They converted to Phantoms in 1974 with FGR2s but exchanged them for FG1s four years later. **Phantom FGR2** XT892/K is at its base, September 1976. Note the folded wings, even on the RAF variant.

Below: Based at Wildenrath, 19 Squadron, along with No. 92, formed the air defence units of the 2nd TAF. Pictured at Fairford in July 1991 is XT899/B, a **Phantom FGR2**. This was the last Phantom to leave the German base when it was delivered in January 1992 to a museum in the Czech Republic.

Below: The grey colour scheme soon absorbed the Phantom fleet. XV500/J, an **FGR2** of 56 Squadron 'The Firebirds', was photographed at Liverpool–Speke in August 1984.

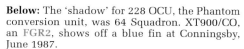

Below: The 'shadow' for 228 OCU, the Phantom conversion unit, was 64 Squadron. XT900/CO, an **FGR2**, shows off a blue fin at Conningsby, June 1987.

Below: A perceived fighter shortage in the RAF led to the acquisition of fifteen former US Navy F4Js in 1984. These were only issued to one unit, as they were very much non-standard aircraft compared with the rest of the RAF fleet, the engine being the main difference. The aircrew even wore standard USN kit. **F4J(UK)** ZE354/R of 74 Squadron is seen at Finningley, September 1989.

Above: From its beginnings as a light-weight fighter the General Dynamics F16 has been developed into a total multi-role attack aircraft that has been sold and is still selling to air forces around the world. The Royal Netherlands Air Force was one of the first four NATO operators (Belgium/Norway/Denmark) to buy the early models. **F16A** J-003 of 306 Squadron is at Mildenhall, May 1995. The task of this unit is tactical reconnaissance.

Below: In 1990 the Portuguese Air Force ordered F16s. Based at Monte Real just one unit, Esq 201, operates the type. **F16A** 15103 is at Fairford, July 1997.

Below: Norway ordered seventy-two Fokker-built F16A and Bs, they are split among four squadrons. **F16A** 670 of Bodø-based 334 Skv is at Fairford, July 1987.

Below: An example of Belgian special colours is this **F16A**, FA115 from 10 Wing. Its markings are to celebrate the fiftieth anniversary of its Kleine Brogel base. It is pictured at Mildenhall, May 1995.

Left: The Belgian Air Force has often painted its aircraft in special markings. **F16A** FA71 of 31 Squadron/10 Wing based at Kleine Brogel shows off very spectacular tiger markings for the NATO Tiger Meet. It is seen at Fairford, July 1998.

Above: Danish Air Force squadron 727 was the first unit in that air arm to receive **F16As** in 1980. E-199 was photographed at Valley in August 1989.

Above: Now in common service with ANG units the F16 operates with more distinctive markings than the regular air force. F16A 82-1023 of 186th FIS Montana ANG is at Reno, NV, September 1988.

Below: The US Marine Corps does not use F16s in squadron formations. It does however participate in the US Navy Fighter Weapons School program (Top Gun) and so has an aircraft in this grey/green colour. F16N 163269 42/NFWS is at London, Ont, June 1990. The F16N was a modified F16C used as an adversary air combat trainer.

Below: This two-seater TF16N is operated by the US Navy 'Top Gun' school. 163279 46/NFWS is seen at London, Ont, June 1990.

Above: Puerto Rico is not a US state but does operate an ANG unit from San Juan. F16A 81-0694 of 198th FS taxies out to take off from its base, November 1992. Note the squadron name 'The Bucaneros' on the intake and the pirate badge behind the cockpit.

Below: Seen at Selfridge ANG base is F16A 80-0505 of 107th TFS Michigan ANG, June 1990. The unit had only finished the transition from A7s a couple of months earlier.

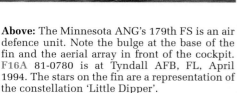
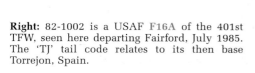

Above: The Minnesota ANG's 179th FS is an air defence unit. Note the bulge at the base of the fin and the aerial array in front of the cockpit. F16A 81-0780 is at Tyndall AFB, FL, April 1994. The stars on the fin are a representation of the constellation 'Little Dipper'.

Right: 82-1002 is a USAF F16A of the 401st TFW, seen here departing Fairford, July 1985. The 'TJ' tail code relates to its then base Torrejon, Spain.

Below: The two-seat conversion trainer for the F16A was the **F16B**. 80-0624 of 161st TFTS/184th FG Kansas ANG is at London, Ont, June 1990. This unit, since deactivated, was a training squadron for ANG F16 pilots.

Above: The **F16C** is the single-seat second-generation aircraft capable of multi-role tasks. 87-0344 of the 63rd FS/ 56th TTW from McDill, FL is at London, Ont, June 1990.

Below: In regular USAF service most F16A units have upgraded to **F16Cs**. Seen departing for a training flight from Fort Wainwright AAF, AK is 90-0745 of the 354th FW, with the blue fin top of the 18th FS. This unit is normally based at Eielson AFB but due to runway resurfacing was operating from the US Army field. It was photographed in May 2000.

Above: In June 1998 **F16D** 91-0464/SP of 22nd FS/52nd FW was seen at Tampere, Finland. This unit is based at Spangdahlem in Germany. The red fin band is the identification for the particular squadron within the wing.

Left: The **Blackburn NA39 Buccaneer** was developed for the Fleet Air Arm as a low-level nuclear strike aircraft. Two de Havilland (later Bristol Siddeley) Gyron Junior engines of 7,100 lb thrust each powered the first variant, the S1. Seen at RNAS Brawdy in July 1963 is XN975 an S.Mk1 of the Aircraft Holding Unit from Lossiemouth. This aircraft, in the short-lived all-white anti-flash colour scheme, was issued the following month to 809 Squadron. It survived its operational life and is preserved at the FAA Museum at Yeovilton. (AG)

Left: The **F16D** is the two-seater variant of the 'C' model. 88-0152/MC of the 63rd FS/56th TTW is at London, Ont, June 1990. Note the cockpit canopy has a gold tint.

Right: The most famous F16 user is the USAF Aerial Demonstration Squadron, better known as 'The Thunderbirds'. **F16A** 81-0663 is seen in the unit's distinctive markings at Reno Cannon, NV, September 1988.

Below: Even before the Buccaneer entered service Blackburn was looking at a more powerful-engined version. The powerplant selected was the Rolls-Royce RB163 Spey of 11,380 lb thrust. The new variant was the S2 and could be spotted by the larger air intakes. XV163 110/E of 800 Squadron based on HMS *Eagle* is seen at Brawdy, August 1968.

Below: The RAF had not wanted the Buccaneer at any price. They were waiting for the TSR2; when it was cancelled they were to get the F111K but this was also cancelled, thus leaving them with Buccaneers. They soon came to appreciate the performance of the aircraft and its ability to fly very low. Buccaneer S2A XV161 of 12 Squadron, the first to be equipped, was seen at Fairford in July 1989.

Above: The Panavia Tornado in its IDS role is the undisputed master of all-weather low-level interdiction and strike operations. Originally known as the MRCA (Multi-Role Combat Aircraft) it has been developed by the industries of Britain, Italy and Germany to equip their attack squadrons. Seen taking off from Fairford in July 1989 is ZA393, a GR1 of the Tornado Weapons Conversion Unit with the 'shadow' numberplate of 45 Squadron.

Below: The RAF's new-build Buccaneers were designated S2Bs, the S2As were converted ex-FAA examples. In 1991 near the end of its service life the aircraft went to war as part of the operation to free Kuwait from the Iraqi invasion forces. The task was to laser-spike targets for the Tornado bombers by operating its Pave Spike to mark targets. On some missions a Buccaneer would both mark and bomb. S2B XV352/U of 208 Squadron was seen in its desert-pink colours at Mildenhall in May 1991, following the war's conclusion.

Below: RAF Tornadoes were used extensively during the Gulf War of 1991. ZA492/GS, a GR1 of 20 Squadron, was photographed at Finningley in September 1991 in its desert-pink colours and missions-flown markings.

Above: The Royal Aircraft Establishment used a number of Buccaneers for various test projects. S2B XW988 was photographed at Fairford in July 1991 in a yellow-and-black scheme.

Left: As the Buccaneer evolved in service various upgrades took place. One was the ability to fire Martel TV-guided air-to-ground missiles. Aircraft so converted were known as S2Ds. XV351 030 of 809 Squadron based on HMS *Ark Royal* heads a line at RNAS Culdrose, August 1974.

Below: The Tornado GR1A is the reconnaissance variant of the type. ZD996 I of 2 Squadron is seen at Mildenhall, May 1993.

Below: No. 27 Squadron was the RAF's third Tornado GR1 unit. In 1985 the squadron took five out of the top six places in the USAF 'Giant Voice' bombing competition. ZA564/JK is at Farnborough in September 1990 in a seventy-fifth anniversary colour scheme.

Above: Tornado GR1 ZD743/CX of 17 Squadron was photographed at Tampere, Finland, in June 1998. This was an RAF Germany unit based at Bruggen. The defence cuts resulted in the disbandment of this unit during March 1999.

Above: The pilot conversion for the Tornado IDS variant took place at RAF Cottesmore at the Tri-National Tornado Training Unit. Aircraft from the UK, Italy and Germany were all based here as well as instructors from each air force. MM7007 I/94 of the Italian Air Force is seen at Valley, August 1987.

Left: In Germany both the air force and the navy fly the Tornado. This *Marineflieger* aircraft, 43+69 of MFG1, shows the early grey and white colour scheme. It is at Fassberg, June 1983.

Below: Italian Tornado MM7070 70-RS of the RSV test wing was photographed in desert colours at Fairford in July 1997.

Right: Seen at its home base of RAF Cottesmore is *Luftwaffe* Tornado 43+04 G/23 of the TTTE June 1987. This unit has since disbanded.

Right: The **Douglas B66 Destroyer** was a light tactical bomber. It was first flown in 1954, having been developed from the navy A3. Seen at Alconbury in May 1964 is 54-0520, an RB66B of the 10th TRW; this was an electronic reconnaissance variant. (AG)

Left: Showing off a special colour scheme at Fairford in July 1999 is 44+88, a *Luftwaffe* **Tornado** of AKG51 'Immelmann'. This IDS unit is based at Schleswig-Jagel.

Below: Saudi Arabia is the only Tornado export country. They operate both the **IDS** and the ADV variant. 762, an IDS of 7 Squadron, is seen at Fairford, July 1995. The home base for this unit is the King Abdullah Aziz Air Base at Dhahran.

Below: This specially marked **Tornado IDS**, 45+79, commemorates the fortieth anniversary of its unit JBG31. It is named *Spirit of Oswald Boelcke*, after a World War I flying ace. It is pictured at Fairford, July 1999.

Above: One variant of the Tornado operated by only the *Luftwaffe* is the ECR. This has an electronic combat, reconnaissance role and is a world-class defence-suppression aircraft. Its task is to seek and destroy enemy radar. 46+45, a **Tornado ECR** of JBG32, is at Fairford, July 1997. The unit's home base is Lechfeld.

Below: The **Lockheed SR71** was one of the most advanced aeroplanes ever built. No longer in service, its performance has never been bettered (by any announced aircraft). It could fly at over 2000 mph; it flew from New York to London in less than two hours and London to Los Angeles in less than four. They were operated by the 9th SRW from Beale AFB, CA. 64-17979 SR71A is at Fairford, July 1985. This airframe is now preserved at Lackland AFB, TX.

Below: Lockheed's earlier reconnaissance platform the U2 is still in service as the TR1 variant. Seen at Edwards AFB is **U2A** 56-6722. This aircraft had over the years been used for various test equipment. Note the skunk on the tail fin. The Lockheed building at Burbank where they were designed is known as 'The Skunk Works'. This airframe has been preserved at the USAF Museum at Dayton, OH.

Left: The Douglas A3D Skywarrior was one of the largest attack aircraft to fly off the US Navy's aircraft carriers. Seen at its home base of Point Magu, CA, is 138938 an NA3B of the PMTC. The 'N' in the type prefix indicates it has been modified as a test aircraft to such an extent as to preclude it reverting to its original state.

Below: The Grumman EA6B Prowler is a four-seat electronic warfare, carrier-based aircraft. It has an enlarged A6 Intruder fuselage. 158542 612/AJ of VAQ 130 is seen onboard USS *Nimitz*, September 1975.

Below: Designed from scratch as a COIN (Counter Insurgency) aircraft the North American Rockwell OV10 Bronco has two seats in tandem and is used in light attack and forward air controller roles. 155438 OV10A ER/12 of VMO-1 'Yazoo' is seen at Hamilton, Ont, June 1990. The aircraft is based at the US Marine Corps station New River, NC.

Below: The OV10A was used by the USAF in the Vietnam War in a forward air control role. 66-13562 of the 20th TASS (Tactical Air Support Squadron) is at Lakenheath, August 1975.

Above: Used by the Colombian Air Force as a light bomber in anti-terrorist and drug-enforcement roles this OV10A, FAC 2216, is on the ramp at Base Aereo Luis F. Gomez at Apiay. Operated by Esc 311, it has live bombs loaded, in this September 1997 picture.

Above: The Victor K2 was the last of the 'V' bombers in service. 55 Squadron disbanded in October 1993 having operated the type from B1 to K2 since 1960. XL190 lands at Fairford in July 1989 trailing its large brake chute. The tanker fleet was by this time in a hemp colour.

Below: Handley Page's crescent-winged Victor bomber was one of Britain's three 'V' bombers. Following its bomber service most were converted to the air-tanking role. Victor K1A XH616 of 57 Squadron is at Leuchars, September 1974.

Above: The Boeing B52 Stratofortress was the big stick of SAC during the cold war. It has been in service since 1955 and is planned to be still operational in 2030, a staggering eighty-five years. B52H 60-0051 of the 93rd BW is in the circuit at its then base Castle AFB, CA in October 1979. The 'H' model was the eighth production variant; it had a shorter tail and TF33 turbofans.

Right: The **B1B** looked very similar to the 'A' but had a number of important differences. The air intakes were modified to reduce radar cross-section and because the new model did not require the Mach-2 performance of the 'A'. One hundred were built for the USAF and the type will serve for many years to come. 86-0123 of the 319th BW based at Grand Forks AFB, North Dakota, is seen flying at Fairford, July 1989.

Below: Seen at Mildenhall, May 1986 is 58-0183, a **B52G** of the 97th BW. No longer in service the 'G' was the first variant with the shorter tail fin. The powerplants were eight Pratt & Whitney J57 turbojets.

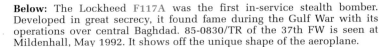

Below: The Lockheed **F117A** was the first in-service stealth bomber. Developed in great secrecy, it found fame during the Gulf War with its operations over central Baghdad. 85-0830/TR of the 37th FW is seen at Mildenhall, May 1992. It shows off the unique shape of the aeroplane.

Above: Planned as a B52 replacement the **Rockwell B1** had a long gestation period. Seen on the ramp at Edwards AFB, October 1979 is the second **B1A** 74-0159 on charge to the AFFTC. US President Jimmy Carter cancelled the project but President Reagan in his arms build up restarted it as the B1B.

Below: The **Fairchild A10** was designed around the GUA-8A Gatling gun. Its role was tank busting and ground attack. Intended for low-level operations, the plane was able to take hits due to having both back-up and armoured parts. 77-0219/DM A10A of the 355th TTW is seen at its base, Davis Monthan AFB, AZ, September 1988.

Above: Seen on the ramp at its base of Borcea-Feteçti is **Harbin H5R** 308 of the 86th Regiment, Romanian Air Force. The H5 is a Chinese-built copy of the Ilyushin IL-28 (Beagle) light bomber. (PJD)

Below: Painted in compass ghost grey is **OA10A** 78-0700/AK of the 354th Wing. The black fin tip indicates it belongs to the 355th FS. Externally identical the OA10 is the 'Fast FAC' (Fast Forward Air Controller). This aircraft was photographed at Fort Wainwright AAF in May 2000 whilst the runway at its home base Eielson AFB was being resurfaced.

Left: The **Sukhoi Su-24** (NATO code-name Fencer) is a long-range low-level Russian attack bomber. With swing-wings and a top speed of Mach 1.35 it is a very formidable warplane. 11(White) was photographed at the Zhukovsky test airfield near Moscow in August 1997. (JDS)

Below: It was late in 1999 that the US Navy retired the **Douglas A4 Skyhawk** from its last task, that of an advanced trainer. The A4 had entered service in 1956 and served in many roles with the USN and Marine Corps. **A4F** 155031 302/UH of VC7 is seen at Edwards AFB, October 1979.

Above: The **A4M** was in fact called the **Skyhawk II** such was its level of upgrades. Most important was a new engine, the P&W J52-P408, which gave a 20% increase in thrust over earlier variants. 160252 3/VL of USMC squadron VMA 331 is seen at Pensacola, October 1981.

Above: Seen at Lemoore NAS, CA, October 1979 is **TA4F** 154334 04/NJ of VA127. The markings were getting less predominant but were still a long way from the all-grey of today.

Above: The **TA4J** was used by the US Navy as an advanced trainer. It was basically an 'F' model with the weapons systems removed. 154291 170/B of training squadron TW2 is at London, Ont, June 1990. It carries the name of USS *Lexington*, the then training carrier.

Above: Ten years after the A4 entered service the two-seat **TA4F** followed. As well as being a trainer it could also carry weapons and was used as a forward air controller (Fast FAC) with the USMC. 154311 4/EX is operated by H&MS 31. This is a Marine Corps HQ and Maintenance squadron. It is pictured at Pensacola, October 1981.

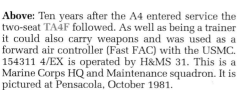

Above: **TA4J** 156946 120/B of VT21 shows the standard red and white US Navy training colours. It is at Pensacola, October 1981.

Right: Australia was one of the countries to buy the Skyhawk. Designated **A4G** they were ex-USN A4Fs, and flew off the ship HMAS *Melbourne*. N13.155051 870 of 805 Squadron RAN is at Greenham Common, June 1977.

Right: The US Navy Flight Demonstration Team, 'The Blue Angels', flew the Skyhawk for nine years from 1974 to 1983. They replaced the F4 Phantom and were in turn replaced by the F/A18 Hornet. **A4F** 154176 No. 6 is seen at Biggs, TX, October 1984. The A4Fs were modified for the team with a number of changes to suit their special role.

Below: Few aircraft have had such a controversial start to life as the swing-wing **General Dynamics F111**. It has matured into an excellent combat-proven weapons system. 67-0101, an **F111A** of the 366th TFW from Mountain Home AFB, is seen at Travis AFB, CA, October 1979.

Above: The next production batch after the F111A was the 'E' model. This was essentially similar but had various updates in the systems. **F111E** 68-0083/UH of the 20th TFW based at Upper Heyford is seen landing at Brawdy, May 1980.

Left: In 1976 America celebrated its bi-centennial. Many aircraft were adorned with special markings for this event. **F111E** 68-0028 of the 20th TFW is at its Upper Heyford base, July 1976.

Above: The **FB111A** was the long-range SAC bomber. It had longer-span wings with extra fuel and revised avionics. 68-0281 of the 380th BW, Plattsburg AFB, NY, is at George AFB, CA, October 1979.

Above: Australia was the only foreign operator of the type and at the current time its only user. **F111C** A8-143 of 6 Squadron, RAAF is seen in flight at Finningley, July 1977.

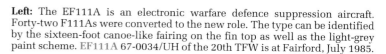

Left: The EF111A is an electronic warfare defence suppression aircraft. Forty-two F111As were converted to the new role. The type can be identified by the sixteen-foot canoe-like fairing on the fin top as well as the light-grey paint scheme. **EF111A** 67-0034/UH of the 20th TFW is at Fairford, July 1985.

Below: The Avro Vulcan was designed as a nuclear-equipped bomber. It was distinctive for its delta shape and the staggering performance at airshows of its fighter-like handling. **Vulcan B1A** XH503 is at Waddington, September 1964. Operated by the Waddington wing, comprised of 44/50/101 Squadrons, the B1A was a B1 with an ECM suite fitted in the tail cone. (AG)

Below: The first service colour of the Vulcans was an anti-flash white. **Vulcan B2** XL387 of 230 OCU was seen at Gaydon in September 1963. (AG)

Below: The **Vulcan B2** had more-powerful engines and increased wingspan. XJ825 of 27 Squadron is at Brawdy, May 1980.

Left: Seen at Leuchars, September 1975 is **Vulcan B2** XM650 of 44 Squadron. The unit badge can be seen on the fin as can the Waddington station badge.

Above: The last **Vulcan** to fly was XH558, a **B2** of the Vulcan Display Team. It operated for eight years after the type was withdrawn from operational service. It was photographed at Boscombe Down in June 1992.

Left: This **Vulcan B2**, XL425 of 617 Squadron 'The Dam Busters', has an all-over camouflage scheme and is a much darker paint than earlier colours. It is seen at Mildenhall, August 1980.

Right: The **KA6D Intruder** is the tanker variant of the type; they are converted from A6A airframes. 151801 520/NK of VA196 was photographed at Lemoore, CA, in October 1979.

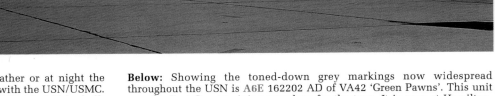

Below: Heading a line of Intruders onboard USS *Nimitz*, September 1975 is **KA6A** 152913 523/AJ of VA35 'Black Panthers'. Large squadron markings such as these are now sadly a thing of the past.

Below: Designed for precision bombing in bad weather or at night the **Grumman A6 Intruder** has operated for many years with the USN/USMC. **A6E** 160424 501/AB of VA34 'Blue Blasters' is at Mildenhall, August 1978.

Below: Showing the toned-down grey markings now widespread throughout the USN is **A6E** 162202 AD of VA42 'Green Pawns'. This unit was the East Coast training squadron for the type. It is seen at Hamilton, Ont, June 1990.

Above: A development of the Cessna T37 trainer, the A37B was a light attack aircraft with eight underwing hard points. It also had more powerful engines and the provision to refuel in flight. It was used operationally by the USAF in Vietnam and also later by ANG units. **A37B** 70-1307 of the AFFTC is at its base of Edwards AFB, October 1979.

Above: The **Tupolev Tu-16** (NATO code-name Badger) was a 1950s vintage Soviet bomber. It is still in service in China where they were built under licence. 57(Red) was photographed at Zhukovsky in August 1995 and features a special modified test nose.

Left: Seen departing Base Aerea Las Palmas, Lima, September 1997 is this **Cessna A37B** 119 of Esc 711. This is the sole unit now flying the type in the Peruvian Air Force. It is based in the north of the country at Piura.

Above: Three **IA-58**s were presented by the Argentine government to the Colombian Air Force. FAC 2202 is seen at Base Aereo Luis F. Gomez at Apiay, September 1997. All had been grounded for lack of spares.

Below: Showing what wonderful colours the US used to operate in is **A7E** 158021 400/NH of VA195. It is at Lemoore, CA, October 1979. The 'E' model was powered by an Allison-built Rolls-Royce Spey engine and had a great number of updates.

Above: The **FMA IA-58 Pucara** is an Argentine designed and built twin turboprop light attack and close support aircraft. As well as guns it has four wing hard points and one under the fuselage. A-19 of the Argentine Air Force is at Farnborough, September 1978.

Above: The conversion trainer for the Corsair II was the TA7C. These were converted 'B' & 'C' models. Showing the two cockpits open is 156795 204/NJ of VA122 (USS *Lexington*), at Lemoore, CA, October 1979.

Above: The commanding officers of navy squadrons always had a more colourful aircraft allocated to them. **A7E** 157516 401/NE belongs to the CO of VA25 based on USS *Ranger*. It was photographed at Lemoore in October 1979.

Below: The US Navy initiated a competition in May 1963 to replace the A4 Skyhawk. The speed of an in-service date was important. The winner was the **LTV A7 Corsair II**. This design was based upon the F8 Crusader but was a smaller aircraft and optimised to be a light bomber rather than a fighter. **A7E** 157522 402/NG of VA147 is at Lemoore, CA, October 1979. This aircraft has 'XO' on the fin top indicating it is used by the squadron executive officer.

Left: The US Navy Air Test Center has an example of practically every type of naval aircraft to operate. **A7E** 156874 405/SD is at its Patuxent River base, May 1989.

Right: One of only seven aircraft converted, 156794 is an **EA7L**. These were TA7Cs converted to be electronic countermeasures platforms. Operated by VAQ34 they acted as an ECM aggressor unit, note the red star on the fin. It was photographed at London, Ont, June 1990.

Above: Seen at Fairford, July 1998 is Greek Air Force **TA7H** 161221. This two-seater is operated by 340 *Mira* from its base at Souda on the island of Crete. The aircraft is used as a fighter-bomber.

Below: USAF orders for the Corsair II came following several years of operational use by the USN. They operated the **A7D**; this variant was then adopted by the navy as the A7E. 73-1002/PT of the 146th TFS Pennsylvania ANG is at Fairford, July 1989.

Above: Once the most colourful of operators, the ANG units with A7s had some of the drabbest markings seen. **A7D** 69-6242 is operated by the 188th FS New Mexico ANG. It is seen at its base, Kirtland AFB, October 1984.

Above: Portugal uses its Corsair IIs in the maritime strike role. **A7P** 5544 (these are refurbished A7As with A7E navigation and attack systems) of Esq 304 is at Conningsby, June 1989. The unit's home base is Monte Real.

Right: **TA7C** 156750 is operated by NAVWPNEVALFAC. This alphabet soup can be broken down to Naval Weapons Evaluation Facility. It is seen at the unit's base Kirtland AFB, NM, October 1984.

Below: Still hanging on in service is the **Meteor D16**. This is a drone variant that can operate without a pilot. Most of the converted aircraft have been shot down in missile tests. WH320 Meteor U16 (now D) N/RAE is seen at its Llanbedr base, July 1969.

Below: In 1944 616 Squadron formed on Gloster Meteor F1s to become Britain's first jet fighter unit. It is amazing that the Meteor is still used today albeit with less than a handful of airframes. **Meteor T7 (Special)** WL419 is operated by Martin-Baker to test ejector seats. Note the open space behind the cockpit. It is seen at Boscombe Down, June 1992.

Left: The **NF13 Meteor** was a tropicalized NF11 night-fighter. WM367 is seen operated by the A&AEE at Boscombe Down, March 1971.

Below: Armstrong Whitworth Aircraft developed the **Meteor TT20** from the NF11 night-fighter variant. The Royal Navy required a shore-based target tug to train gunners and guided missile operators. WM255 of the Fleet Requirement Unit is at its Hurn base, April 1968.

Above: The **English Electric Canberra** seems to have an unlimited life span. First flown in May 1949 it still serves today. XH135 is a **PR9** AG/ of 1 PRU (39 Squadron). It is seen at West Malling, August 1989. The PR9 version is still an efficient and very high-flying photo reconnaissance platform.

Above: The two-seat **Meteor** trainer was the **T7**. It is of note that this aircraft did not have ejector seats. WA662 is operated by the RAE in this smart colour scheme. It is seen at Finningley, September 1984.

Left: The last of the single-seat **Meteor** fighters was the **F8**. WH453 is seen at Woodvale, September 1971 on charge to No. 5 CAACU (Civilian Anti-Aircraft Co-operation Unit). This unit was tasked with providing target practice for ack-ack gunners.

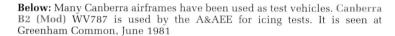

Below: Many Canberra airframes have been used as test vehicles. **Canberra B2 (Mod)** WV787 is used by the A&AEE for icing tests. It is seen at Greenham Common, June 1981

Below: The German *Luftwaffe* operated three **Canberra B2s** as test aircraft. 99+35 of the MilGeoAMT departs Greenham Common, July 1983 in bright orange markings.

Right: To celebrate the fiftieth anniversary of the first flight of the Canberra, the RAF painted **T4** WJ874 as VN799, the first prototype. Used as a trainer for 39 Squadron pilots it is seen just about to touch down at Fairford, July 1999.

Above: No. 231 OCU was the conversion unit for the Canberra for many years. WT480/B, a **T4**, is at its Cottesmore base, May 1972.

Above: Seen at Leuchars, September 1974 is **Canberra T19** WJ975/X of 100 Squadron, a target facilities unit. The T19 was a T11 that had had the radar removed as well as various other changes.

Above: A unique unit in the RAF, 360 Squadron was formed as recently as October 1966, not having a wartime record. A joint RAF/RN unit, it was tasked with electronic countermeasures training. **Canberra T17** WJ981/S is seen at Leuchars, September 1975.

Below: So successful a design was the Canberra that the USAF ordered it for the interdiction role. Built by the Glen L. Martin company of Baltimore, it was designated B57. **EB57E** 55-4263 is seen at Binbrook, August 1978. Operated by the 17th DSES (Defence Systems Evaluation Squadron) it was one of five to visit Europe for exercises.

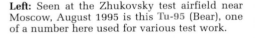

Left: Seen at the Zhukovsky test airfield near Moscow, August 1995 is this **Tu-95** (Bear), one of a number here used for various test work.

Above: The Tupolev **Tu-160** (NATO code-name Blackjack) is the largest bomber in the world today. It has swing-wings and a similar configuration to the B1B but is far larger. Its wing span is nearly fifty-foot wider and the fuselage thirty-foot longer. 29(Black) in a half-painted state lines up to take off at Zhukovsky, August 1995.

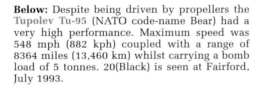

Below: Despite being driven by propellers the **Tupolev Tu-95** (NATO code-name Bear) had a very high performance. Maximum speed was 548 mph (882 kph) coupled with a range of 8364 miles (13,460 km) whilst carrying a bomb load of 5 tonnes. 20(Black) is seen at Fairford, July 1993.

Below: The first American supersonic bomber was the **Convair B58 Hustler**. It had a short operational life, entering service in 1960 and being withdrawn in 1970. 59-2440 B58A of the 64th BS/43rd BW is seen at Mildenhall, May 1969. The home base for the aircraft was Carswell AFB.

Above: The **Boeing RB47H** was an electronic reconnaissance variant of the original B47 six-engined bomber. 53-4280 is seen at Upper Heyford, May 1967. Note that the serial has the 'O' prefix. This was to indicate the aircraft was over ten years old. This procedure has since been dropped as the life of military aircraft has grown to figures that would not have been believed at one time. (AG)

Below: Looking like a set square in the sky, **B2B** 82-1069 is seen over Fairford, July 1999.

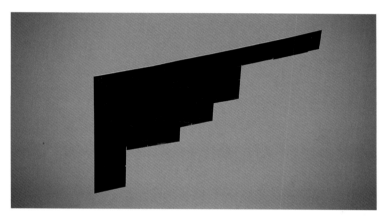

Above: With wings still spread **Tu-160** 29 (Black) climbs away before beginning its flying display at Zhukovsky, August 1995.

Above: Russian **Tu-22M3** 9804 is seen here about to take off at Zhukovsky, August 1995.

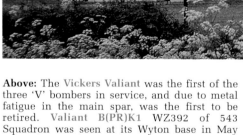

Below: The **Northrop B2A** bomber is today the most advanced and expensive warplane in service. It is a flying wing with very high stealth capability. 82-1069/WM of the 393rd BS/ 509th BW is seen landing at Fairford, July 1999.

Above: The **Vickers Valiant** was the first of the three 'V' bombers in service, and due to metal fatigue in the main spar, was the first to be retired. **Valiant B(PR)K1** WZ392 of 543 Squadron was seen at its Wyton base in May 1964, along with two others. (AG)

Below: Making its first appearance in the west was this Russian **Tu-22M3** (Backfire C) c/n 12112347. It is pictured on a landing approach at the Farnborough airshow, September 1992.

Right: The Tupolev Tu-22 has been used to designate two very different bombers. First was the 'Blinder' range and then the much more formidable 'Backfire'. This latter aircraft is a supersonic swing-wing strategic bomber. 57(Red) is a **Tu-22M3** operated by 185 Regiment, Ukrainian Air Force. When the Soviet Union split up, most of the states took possession of any equipment on their soil. It is pictured at Fairford, July 1998.

Below: As the name would imply the **Super Etendard** is an upgrade of the earlier version. No. 60 of French Navy squadron 11F is at Boscombe Down, June 1992.

Below: The Dassault Etendard IV is a single-place carrier-based strike aircraft with a transonic performance. A number were built as photo reconnaissance variants with the designation IVP. **Etendard IVP** No. 106 is operated by French Navy squadron 16F. It is seen at Chivenor, August 1970.

Above: The **Dassault Mirage IV** is a French supersonic bomber, and was operated by the *Force de Frappe* to deliver a nuclear payload. The only version still in service is the **IVP**, a PR aircraft. No. 55/CB is operated by EB1/91 and based at Mont-de-Marsan. It is pictured at Fairford, July 1994.

Below: For nearly forty years the **North American Rockwell T2 Buckeye** has been training pilots for the US Navy. **T2C** 642/C 158327 of training squadron VT26 is pictured at Pensacola, October 1981. The home base is Chase Field, TX.

Above: Painted in special markings to celebrate seventy-five years of US Navy aviation, **T2C Buckeye** 158602 of CTW 2 is seen visiting Oshkosh, WI, August 1986.

Below: The **Lockheed T33 Shooting Star** has been training pilots around the world for many years. **T33A** 56-1782 of the AFTC was photographed at McGuire AFB in August 1970. (SGW)

Above: The Portuguese Air Force used the T33 from 1957 to 1976. 1920 is seen at Upper Heyford, June 1971. This aircraft was operated by BA1 at Sintra.

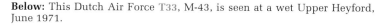

Below: This Dutch Air Force T33, M-43, is seen at a wet Upper Heyford, June 1971.

Below: Colombia was the first country in South America to operate the T33, the first were in service in 1954. T33A FAC 2020 is at Madrid AFB near Bogotá, September 1997.

Above: West Germany's first post-war generation of pilots were trained in the T33. 9500 is seen at Greenham Common, July 1974.

Below: In Canada the T33 is known as the CT133 Silverstar. 133119 of 414 Squadron, a combat support unit, is seen in special markings for the seventy-fifth anniversary of the Canadian Air Force. The unit is based at Comox, BC where it is pictured, May 2000.

Above: The US Navy variant of the T33 was the TV2. As can be seen, the area behind the cockpit is quite different. The aircraft is also equipped with a tail hook. 144204 7W is the base flight aircraft at Willow Grove, August 1970. (SGW)

Left: This Ecuadorian Air Force T33A FAE 806 was seen at Latacunga AFB in September 1997.

Below: The Bolivian Air Force replaced the last of its F86 Sabres with T33s. *Grupo Aereo de Caza* 32 operates them. T33 FAB 635 is at El Trompillo, Santa Cruz, November 1992.

Below: Following the success of the Aermacchi MB326 the company developed the MB339, a two-seat, in-tandem, advanced jet trainer. Seen here is **MB339A** MM54507 55/ of the SVBIA. This unit is an Italian Air Force flying school then based at Lecce Galatina. It was photographed at Valley in August 1985.

Above: The **Mudry CAP 20** is a single-seat aerobatic aircraft. Designed for +8 and -6 G, it was acquired in small numbers by the French Air Force for aerobatic practice. No. 6/VZ is at Reims, May 1983.

Below: The **Canadair CT114 Tutor** is a two-seat side-by-side basic jet trainer. It is only in service in Canada. 114163 is operated by the Central Flying School for instructor training. It is pictured at its Winnipeg base in June 1990.

Below: Officially known as 431 Air Demonstration Squadron, to the Canadian public they are better known as 'The Snowbirds' aerobatic team. **CT114 Tutor** 114049 is the team's No. 11 aircraft. It is seen at London, Ont, June 1990. The team is based at Moose Jaw, Saskatchewan.

Above: The **Aermacchi MB339C** is a slightly larger variant optimised to be a lead-in fighter trainer or a light attack aircraft in its own right. NZ6469 of 14 Squadron RNZAF at Boscombe Down in June 1992, prior to delivery. The home base is Ohakea on North Island.

Below: The **Aermacchi MB339AP** is operated by the Peruvian Air Force Academy. They are used by Esc 513 for advanced training. 485 leads a line of three at the unit's base, Las Palmas, September 1997.

Below: The **TC4C Academe** is based upon the airframe of the Grumman G159 Gulfstream 1 twin-prop executive transport. This US Navy aircraft has a new nose into which is fitted the radar from the A6 Intruder. In the cabin there are locations for training the navigator/bombardier. 155722 850/NJ of VA128 is seen at London, Ont, June 1990.

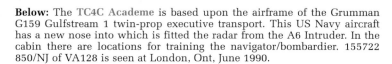

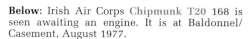

Below: Irish Air Corps **Chipmunk T20** 168 is seen awaiting an engine. It is at Baldonnel/ Casement, August 1977.

Above: The de Havilland (Canada) DHC1 Chipmunk was a single-engined, tandem-seat, basic trainer for the RAF. **Chipmunk T10** WP896 is operated by 10 AEF (Air Experience Flight). It is seen at its Woodvale base, May 1984.

Below: A joint venture between Dornier and Dassault resulted in the Alpha Jet. It is used by the French as an advanced trainer. **Alpha Jet E** E140 314-VV is operated by EAC 314 from Tours. It was photographed at Valley in August 1983.

Below: Belgium uses its **Alpha Jets** in the advanced training role. They however frequently paint aircraft in very distinctive colour schemes. AT29 is operated by 9 Wing. It is seen at Conningsby, June 1989.

Below: France's national aerobatic team the 'Patrouille de France' flies the **Alpha Jet E.** E174 No. 1 is seen at Abbotsford, BC, August 1986. The team is based at Salon-de-Provence.

Below: The Germans have used the Alpha Jet in the light attack role where they replaced the Fiat G91. **Alpha Jet A** 41+27 of JBG 43 is seen at Cottesmore, June 1987.

Below: The **Embraer EMB 312 Tucano** is a very successful Brazilian turboprop, tandem-seat trainer. The Brazilian Air Force aerobatic team *Escuadron de Fumaca* or Smoke Squadron operates it. **Tucano T27** FAB 1311 is airborne at Abbotsford, BC, August 1986.

Above: The Colombian Air Force bought fourteen **T27 Tucanos** and operates them as both trainers and light attack aircraft, utilising the underwing hard points. FAC 2263 of Esc 312 was photographed at its base, Luis F. Gomez, at Apiay in September 1997.

Right: The order for the new RAF trainer to replace the Jet Provost was one of the most hotly contested of recent years. The winner was the Tucano. The version chosen by the RAF is built by Shorts and has a more powerful Garrett TPE 331-12B engine. Tucano T1 ZF447 of 3 FTS is seen at Mildenhall, May 1993.

Above: Between flying F4 Phantoms and the current F16s the USAF aerobatic team 'The Thunderbirds' flew T38A Talons. No. 5 is seen at Harlingen, TX, October 1979. This unit is exceptional in not always showing a full aircraft serial.

Above: The French Air Force is one of the latest customers for the Tucano having placed orders for eighty. EMB 312F No. 469 312-JN is from flying school GI.00.312 at Salon-de-Provence. It is seen at Fairford, July 1999.

Below: The T38B is a reconfigured T38A fitted with hard points to be a 'lead-in fighter trainer' (LIFT). 65-10457/HM is operated in this role by 434th TTS/479th TTW based at Holloman AFB, NM. It was photographed in October 1984, at Biggs AAF base, TX.

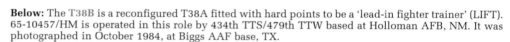

Above: In service since 1961 and with life extensions for perhaps twenty more years, the Northrop T38 Talon will by the time it is replaced have provided advanced flying training to several generations of American pilots. 64-13235/VN of the 71st FTW Vance AFB is seen at Hamilton, Ont, June 1990.

Below: To expand the learning curve of navy test pilots a T38B, 60-0582, has been added to the USNTPS fleet. The USN has of course not operated the type for normal training. It is seen at Patuxent River, MD, May 1989.

Below: Turkey is one of the few countries to operate the T38. It is used as an advanced trainer. 38227 (2-227) of 2 AJU is seen at its base of Izmir Cigli, May 1998. (PJD)

Left: The Folland Gnat was originally a single-seat lightweight fighter that was developed into the Gnat T1 two-seat advanced trainer. First flown in 1959 it entered service with the CFS in 1962 and later the same year with 4 FTS at Valley. This unit provided all RAF fast jet pilots with advanced training. Gnat T1 XS104 of 44/4 FTS is at its base, August 1968.

Below: The BAe Hawk has been a great export success. Designed as a replacement for the Gnat the first aircraft were received at the end of 1976. Hawk T1 XX177 of 4 FTS is seen at its Valley base, August 1977.

Above: As well as an advanced flying training role the Hawk could also operate as a weapons trainer. Hawk T1 XX327/B of 2 TWU (Tactical Weapons Unit) with the shadow markings of 151 Squadron was photographed at Valley in August 1983, in its war-like camouflage colours.

Above: In the grey colour scheme is Hawk T1A XX263 of 2 TWU with its second shadow unit, 63 Squadron. It is seen at North Weald, May 1992.

Above: Hawk T1 XX235 of 74(R) Squadron was seen at Fairford, July 1996, in special airshow markings. This reserve unit is part of 4 FTS at Valley.

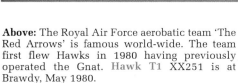

Above: The Royal Air Force aerobatic team 'The Red Arrows' is famous world-wide. The team first flew Hawks in 1980 having previously operated the Gnat. Hawk T1 XX251 is at Brawdy, May 1980.

Above: The station flight at RAF St Athan painted this Hawk T1, XX172, with the Welsh Dragon. It is seen at Fairford, July 1995.

Right: The Hawk is used by the Finnish Air Force as both a trainer and as an attack fighter. All commands have a Hawk flight attached. Hawk Mk51 HW348/A is operated by the 3rd Flight of the 31st Fighter Squadron at Rissala. It was photographed at its base in June 1998.

Below: In the air force of South Korea the Hawk is used in a dual role for advanced flying and as a weapons trainer. **Hawk T67** 67-496 is seen at Warton, August 1992, prior to delivery to the 216th TCS/8th TCW at Wongiu.

Above: A tribute to the quality of the Hawk's design was the decision by the US Navy to operate it as an advanced carrier-borne trainer. It is being licence-built by McDonnell Douglas as the **T45 Goshawk**. A great deal of engineering work had to be done to make the aircraft seaworthy. 162788 T45A 2/NATC is seen under test at Patuxent River, MD, May 1989.

Above: The de Havilland Vampire was first flown in 1943 and entered service with the RAF three years later. It was widely exported to over twenty different air arms. The last major user of the type was the Swiss Air Force who used both single and two-seater aircraft in the advanced flying training role. **Vampire FB6** J-1183 is at Dübendorf, August 1987.

Above: For nearly twenty-five years RAF multi-engined pilot training has been conducted by the Handley Page (Now BAe) Jetstream. **Jetstream T1** XX500/H of 6 FTS is seen at its then base Finningley, September 1990.

Above: The two-seat Vampire was in a side-by-side configuration. U-1214, a **Vampire T55** of the Swiss Air Force, is at Dübendorf, August 1987.

Above: The last user of the Vampire in the RAF was the Central Flying School. This unit's role is to train flying instructors. **Vampire T11** XK624 32/CFS is at Coltishall, September 1971.

Right: The Jetstream T3 as operated by the Royal Navy for Observer (Navigator) training is a far more up-to-date aircraft than its RAF counterpart. It has new engines (Garrett TPE 331 turboprops) and is based upon the successful Jetstream 31 airliner. **Jetstream T3** ZE439 577/Yeovilton Station Flight was photographed at its base in July 1994.

Left: The **Fouga CM170 Magister** is a widely used trainer/light attack aircraft. It has a distinctive 'V'-shaped tail. Unlike many of its contemporaries it has two engines albeit low powered (880 lb/400 kg thrust Turbomeca Marbore 11A turbojets). Illustrated is 215 of the Irish Air Corps at Baldonnel/Casement in August 1977. A total of six was obtained and could be used to fire rockets.

Below: Being the designers and builders of the type the French Air Force has been the largest user of the **Magister**. No. 11/AR is at Châteaudun, June 1977.

Above: The Irish Air Corps' only jet equipment for many years was the two-seat Vampire trainer. 192, a **T55**, is at its base HQ Baldonnel/Casement, July 1971. (SGW)

Below: Belgium's aerobatic team '*Diables Rouges*' (Red Devils) flew the **CM170** until they were disbanded. MT15 lands at Leuchars, September 1974 following a display.

Below: This French Air Force example is in spectacular marks for the NATO Tiger Meet. **CM170R** No. 572/AD of GI.312 is at Fairford, July 1991.

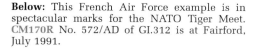

Below: The Belgian Air Force used the **Stampe SV4B** until 1971, making it the last European basic trainer biplane in service. V28 is at Biggin Hill, May 1968. (SGW)

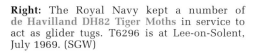

Above: The Piper Super Cub was developed in 1950 from the L4 Cub. They were used by the military as army spotter planes. Still in the service with the Belgian Air Force is this **L21B Super Cub** LB-05. Its current use is that of a glider tug for air cadets. It is pictured at Brustem, September 1996. (SGW)

Right: The Royal Navy kept a number of de Havilland DH82 Tiger Moths in service to act as glider tugs. T6296 is at Lee-on-Solent, July 1969. (SGW)

Right: With its shoulder-mounted wing, the SAAB 105 is quite a distinctive trainer and light attack aircraft. It has side-by-side seating and twin engines. As well as its native Sweden it has been sold to the Austrians. **SAAB 105OE** GF-16 is operated by 3 Flight Regiment, Austrian Air Force. It is seen with a tiger-marked tail at Fairford, July 1997.

Above: Until the delivery in May 1988 of the SAAB Draken the sharp end of the Austrian Air Force was the **SAAB 105OE**. In the last few years they have abandoned any attack role and have reverted to being trainers. 1110/J (Yellow) is at North Weald, May 1972.

Below: Sweden's aerobatic unit 'Team 60' flew the **SAAB 105**. The unit is seen lined up at Boscombe Down, June 1992 with 60096 at the start of the row. The only extra markings for the team was the repainted tail, the fuselage being in normal drab green.

Above: The **Jet Provost T4** had a more powerful Bristol Siddeley Viper engine, giving it 40% more thrust than the T3. This rare camouflaged example, XR679 of 04/TWU/79 Squadron, is used to train forward air controllers hence its war-like colours. It is pictured at Valley, August 1983.

Above: A side-by-side two-seat primary trainer, the **Piaggio P148** first flew in 1951 and served with the Italian Air Force. MM53736 RR92 is at Venice Lido, September 1966. (SGW)

Left: Seen at its Little Rissington base in August 1964 is **Jet Provost T3** XM360 71/CFS. This two-seat basic trainer was designed to give 'ab initio' courses for would-be pilots. The first such course for the RAF started in September 1959. (AG)

Above: A redesigned hood is the feature to distinguish the **Jet Provost T5**; this is because it was the first variant to be pressurised. 'The Poachers' aerobatic team from RAF College Cranwell operates XW336 6/RAFC. The college uses the light-blue tail band as a unit marker. It was photographed at Valley in August 1973.

Below: The **Hunting Percival Provost** was adopted in 1953 as the Royal Air Force's standard basic trainer. A single 550 hp Alvis Leonides air-cooled radial piston engine powered it. **Provost T Mk1** XF896 05/CFS is seen at its base, Little Rissington, August 1964. (AG)

Above: Derived from the Jet Provost the **BAC167 Strikemaster** was an economical way to give a low-tech air arm firepower. It had fixed machine-guns and four hard points able to take an assorted load. Seen prior to delivery at Hurn, July 1969 is **Strikemaster Mk81** 501 of the Yemen Arab Republic Air Force. This aircraft and the other three ordered were sold on in the early 1970s to Singapore. (SGW)

Left: Bought new, the Irish Air Corps operated Provost T51s and T53s. Delivered in 1953–4 they remained in service as trainers until the 1970s. **Provost T53** 183 is at its Baldonnel/Casement base, July 1971. (SGW)

Above: The Spanish Air Force **T35 Tamiz** is a CASA-assembled Enaer T35 Pillan. This is a Chilean designed and built basic trainer. It is used in this role in Spain before pilots progress to the CASA 101. E26-25 79-72 of EVE (Elementary Flying School) is at its base, San Javier, April 1994. (PJD)

Below: Following the demise of Beagle Aircraft production of the Bulldog primary side-by-side trainer was taken over by Scottish Aviation. It was ordered by the RAF to replace the Chipmunk, 132 were obtained. The main users within the RAF were the University Air Squadrons. **Bulldog T1** XX638 of 3FTS is in the latest black colour scheme at Cottesmore, June 1996.

Above: The **Soko G4 Super Galeb** is one of the many advanced trainer/ light attack aircraft on the market today. However, since it is built in what was once Yugoslavia it has very little chance of gaining any more sales. 23693 is in the colours of 'Letece Zvezde' (Flying Stars), the aerobatic team of the Yugoslavian Air Force. It is seen on a visit to an airshow in the Czech Republic at Hradec Králové, August 1998. (PJD)

Above: Of Czech origin, the **Aero L29 Delfin** was the standard jet trainer for the whole of the Warsaw Pact group. Over 3000 were built. It had many roles from basic to advanced to weapons trainer. 2330 L29 of the Czech Air Force VZLU is at Hradec Králové, August 1998. (SGW)

Right: In the Romanian Air Force training for both air and ground duties is provided at the SMOA (Institute for Aviation) at Boboc. Seen at its base, May 1999 is **Aero L29** 54(Red). (PJD)

Left: Pilots from the National Air Academy fly in secondary duties for the Spanish Air Force aerobatic unit '*Team Aguila*'. Their mounts are these specially painted **CASA 101 Aviojets**. This is another of the advanced trainer/light attack designs available to air arms of the world. As well as Spain, Jordan, Chile and Honduras operate it. E25.22 79-22 lines up to take off at Fairford, July 1995.

Above: The USAF entered the **Cessna T37** basic jet side-by-side trainer into service in 1957. The aircraft is powered by two 1025 lb (465 kg) thrust Continental J69 turbojets. Seen on the ramp at Williams Gateway, AZ, in October 1998 is 58-1956/XL **T37B** of the 85th TFS/47th TFW from Laughlin AFB, TX.

Above: The 'C' model of the T37 has provision for both tip tanks, for extra fuel, and to be able to carry weapons. **T37C** 2406 of the Portuguese Air Force aerobatic team '*Asas de Portugal*' is at Fairford, July 1989.

Above: The **North American Harvard/Texan** can claim to be the most important and perhaps widely used training aircraft ever. Powered by a single 550 hp P&W Wasp air-cooled radial engine it first entered service in 1938 and can still be found in service today. Two are used by the A&AEE at Boscombe Down as low-speed chase aircraft for trials. **Harvard T2B** KF183 basks in the type's reflected glory at Fairford, July 1987.

Above: The light aircraft subsidiary of Aerospatiale (SOCATA) designed the **TB30 Epsilon** trainer to have the layout of instruments and handling characteristics of the Alpha Jet. This plan would ease the pilot from basic to advanced trainer as painlessly as possible. As well as French use it has been sold to the Portuguese Air Force, which had the airframes assembled in country by OGMA. 11409 of Esq 101 is seen at its Beja base, March 1997. (PJD)

Below: Turkey is one of the countries to adopt the T37 as its basic trainer. **T37B** 88074/2.074 of 2 AJU is seen at its Cigu base, May 1998. The 'B' variant of the T37 had more powerful engines as well as improved navigation systems. All 'A' models were brought up to 'B' standard. (PJD)

Above: To replace the Harvard in Swiss Air Force service the Pilatus company designed the P3 trainer. It entered service in 1955 but has since been replaced in the training role by the PC7. Some can still be found as station flight aircraft. **Pilatus P3** A-810 is at Locarno, July 1970.

Below: With a P&W (Canada) PT6 turboprop as a powerplant the **Pilatus PC7** is a great leap forward in training technology over the P3. In service with at least seventeen air forces, it can also be fitted with hard points under the wings for weapons training or as a light attack aircraft. A-903 is seen at the Swiss Air Force base of Dübendorf, August 1987.

Above: Seen in the well-known red/white training colours is **T28B** 137775 E/446 of TW5. This US Navy aircraft is seen visiting Harlingen, TX, October 1979

Below: With the delivery in 1989 of a fleet of thirteen **Pilatus PC7s** the Royal Dutch Air Force resumed basic training of its military pilots, army, navy and air force. Prior to this they had a joint venture with the Belgians and the Canadians. L-09 PC7 of EMVO (Elementary Flying Training Squadron) based at Woensdrecht, is seen at Fairford, July 1995.

Below: The US Army was not a regular Trojan operator but several examples have found their way into army service for trials and chase duties. **T28B** (1)37747 is at London, Ont, June 1990.

Below: North American, who had built the T6 Harvard/Texan won the competition to replace it in the USAF. This was the **T28 Trojan**. Following two years' air force service it was selected by the US Navy. They operated the T28B with a 1425 hp Wright R1830 Cyclone radial piston engine. This was 650 hp more than the USAF T28A. **T28B** 138271 094/NJ of VA122 is at Lemoore, CA, October 1979.

Above: India in a desire to adopt a local design for its requirement of a basic jet trainer produced the **Hindustan HJT-16 Kiran**. It first flew in 1964 and was quite advanced having zero altitude Martin-Baker ejector seats and cabin pressurisation. U2462 is seen at the Farnborough Air Show, September 1964 on a sales trip.

Right: The **Pitts S2A Special** is a small, very advanced, aerobatic biplane. It is mainly to be found in the private market place but for a period of time the Chilean Air Force operated an aerobatic team of five. These were known as 'The Halcones'. 2231 leads the team line up at Fairford, July 1989.

Below: In the competition for the Warsaw Pact jet trainer contract the **PZL TS-11 Iskra** lost out to the L29 Delfin. It was however put into production by the Polish Air Force; the only other sale was to India. 709 No. 8 of the Polish Air Force aerobatic team 'White Iskras' lands at Fairford, July 1995.

Above: The new Polish Air Force basic trainer was developed from an abandoned piston-engined project. This is the **PZL 130 Turbo Orlik** (Spotted Eaglet). 036 from 60 LPS (Air School Regiment) lands at Fairford, July 1998.

Above: The Finnish **Valmet L70 Vinka** is designed and built in-country, to fulfil the role of basic trainer. It first flew in December 1979 with deliveries starting in October the following year. They have not been sold to any other country. VN-7 is pictured in June 1998 on charge to the Air Academy at Kauhava.

Above: Valmet in Finland has added a new, more powerful trainer to its stable with the **L90TP Redigo**. This features a 500 shp Allison turboprop together with a retractable undercarriage. RG-4 is seen at Rissala, June 1998, where it is operated by the 4th Flight (Communications) of the 31st Fighter Squadron.

Below: The **Boeing Stearman 75 Kaydet** was a radial piston-engined biplane trainer that first entered US Army Air Force service as the **PT13** in 1936. This example, FAB 16, was still in use in November 1992 by the Bolivian Air Force at Santa Cruz. It is not so much used as a trainer but more as a great toy by the pilots lucky enough to fly it.

Above: The current basic trainer for the Bolivian Air Force is the **Aerotec A122A Uirapura**. This aircraft is a Brazilian design powered by a 160 hp Lycoming piston engine. The Primary Squadron of the College of Military Aviation at Santa Cruz operates FAB 174. It was photographed in November 1992.

Below: In a major change to its flying training policy the USAF now separates pilots after T37 flying and only people destined for fast jets go on to T38s. The pilots destined for transport aircraft now go on to learn their advanced flying on the **Beech T1A Jayhawk**. This twinjet was purchased as an 'off the shelf' design and in civil life is the Beechjet 400. 92-0339/RA T1A is operated by the 99th FTS/12th FTW at Randolph AFB, TX. It is pictured at Tyndall AFB, FL, April 1994.

Above: Most **Cessna 150s** in the world can be found in civil flying clubs teaching the private pilot how to fly. A few can be found in military colours. FAE 503 is operated by the Ecuadorian Air Force at its training school at Salinas. It was photographed in September 1997.

Below: Currently operated by the King Faisal Air Academy at Al Kharj, the Royal Saudi Air Force flies Cessna FR172s. 618 is seen prior to delivery at Hurn, April 1968.

Above: To train its navigators the Canadian Armed Forces have adapted the popular de Havilland (Canada) – now Bombardier – DHC8 Dash 8 short-haul airliner. To do this they have added mapping radar in an extended nose. CT142 142804 of the Air Navigation School was at its Winnipeg base in June 1990.

Below: The main task of Primary Instruction Squadron 511 of the Peruvian Air Force is self-evident from its name. However, one of its aircraft is pictured here with the door removed as it taxies to take off with two parachutists in the back. Cessna T41 416 is at its Las Palmas base, September 1997.

Below: In 1973 a T34 with a turboprop was initiated and later that year one of two modified aircraft flew with a P&W PT6 of some 715 shp. A total of 352 new-build T34Cs were obtained by the US Navy. 161821 721/G of training squadron VT27 is at Biggs AAF, TX, October 1984. The unit is based at NAS Corpus Christi, TX.

Below: Being part of the army the Irish Air Corps has an Army Co-operation Squadron based at Baldonnel/Casement. They fly the French-built Reims (Cessna) FR172 for duties such as target towing, parachuting and surveillance. 207 is seen at its base, August 1977.

Below: The SIAI-Marchetti SF260 is a fully aerobatic basic trainer that can also be used in an armed counter-insurgency role. The Belgian Air Force obtained the type in 1969 to replace the Stampe SV4 and they serve to this day. SF260MB ST-32 from 5 SMA/1 Wing, Beauvechain is seen at Fairford, July 1989.

Left: The Beech T34B Mentor was a US Navy primary trainer powered by a 225 hp Continental piston engine. (The USAF had used the 'A' model.) Some 423 were delivered by 1957. 144044 is seen at Pensacola, October 1981 with 'Fly Navy' titles. This is one of many T34Bs used by Recruiting Command (part of Training Command). They are used to fly potential recruits to see if they have problems with flying such as airsickness before they get on to an expensive training syllabus.

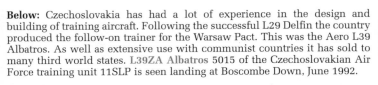

Below: Czechoslovakia has had a lot of experience in the design and building of training aircraft. Following the successful L29 Delfin the country produced the follow-on trainer for the Warsaw Pact. This was the Aero L39 Albatros. As well as extensive use with communist countries it has sold to many third world states. **L39ZA Albatros** 5015 of the Czechoslovakian Air Force training unit 11SLP is seen landing at Boscombe Down, June 1992.

Above: Among Ecuador's armed forces both the air force and the navy operate **T34Cs**. FAE 0019 is an air force example operated by the Air Force Flying School at Salinas. It is pictured at its base, September 1997.

Below: In a far brighter colour scheme is this Ecuadorian Navy **T34C**. ANE 221 is at the navy's only base, Guayaquil, September 1997. None of the aircraft operated by the navy has an offensive capability.

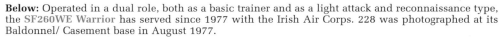

Above: Lithuania emerged from the Soviet Union as the first of the three Baltic States to regain its independence. It has a very small air force with aircraft mainly donated by neighbouring states. Four **L39C Albatros** jets were purchased from the former Soviet republic of Kyrgyzstan and they are operated by 11 Squadron at Zokniai. 02(Blue) is seen at its base, May 1995. (JDS)

Below: Operated in a dual role, both as a basic trainer and as a light attack and reconnaissance type, the **SF260WE Warrior** has served since 1977 with the Irish Air Corps. 228 was photographed at its Baldonnel/ Casement base in August 1977.

Above: Romania's Institute of Aviation (SMOA) at Boboc operates the **L39ZA** in the advanced training role. 132(Red) is seen at its base, May 1999. (PJD)

Right: The **Lockheed C130 Hercules** is without a doubt the finest and most widely used military transport in use today. First flown in 1954 it is still in production. The USAF is the biggest operator of the type and uses it for a very wide range of tasks. 63-7767 C130E is seen at Odiham in September 1964 in the early all-silver colour. (AG)

Below: The HC130P is a combat aircrew rescue aeroplane. It is an upgrade of the HC130N having a larger radome amongst other changes. 66-0224 HC130P of the 129th Rescue Squadron California ANG is at its then base Heywood, October 1979. The following year the unit moved to Moffett NAS.

Above: On-type training for the Air National Guard is provided by the 154th TATS of the Arkansas ANG. C130E 62-1784 is at Reno, NV, September 1988.

Left: This Hercules is an EC130E 'Rivet Rider', a special variant that can intercept and re-broadcast both radio and television programmes. This can be used in civil emergencies to broadcast news or in a wartime operation for psychological warfare and propaganda. Note the antennas on the fin and the large underwing pods. 63-9816 is operated by the 193rd SOS of the Pennsylvania ANG. It is pictured at Fairford, July 1998.

Below: The designation NC130A indicates that the aircraft is a C130A used for permanent test work and could not be converted back if required. (A 'J' prefix is a temporary modification.) NC130A 55-0022 of the 4950th Test Wing Air Force Systems Command from Wright Patterson AFB, OH is seen at London, Ont, June 1990.

Above: Armed with a 105 mm Howitzer as well as 20 and 40 mm cannons the AC130 Gun Ship packs a tremendous punch as a ground-attack aircraft. Such aeroplanes evolved during the Vietnam War starting with AC47s then AC119s before the AC130. Within the Hercules range there have been the AC130A/E/H versions, each one an improvement on the previous. AC130H 69-6572 is at Edwards AFB, CA, October 1979.

Left: Based at Kirtland AFB, NM, the 1550th Aircrew Training and Test Wing was tasked with training in the specialist art of combat rescue. HC130P 66-0212 of the unit is seen at Biggs AAF, TX, October 1984.

Right: The WC130H was a conversion for the Air Weather Service of the HC130H. WC130H 65-0972 of the 920th Weather Reconnaissance Group is at Harlingen, TX, October 1979.

Below: Full colour markings together with a red tail on this **LC130H** of the 139th TAS, New York Air National Guard, indicate a special role. This is supporting the DEW Line radar system in the Arctic regions hence the skis fitted to the undercarriage. It was photographed at Fairford in July 1994.

Below: **C130A** 54-1640 is operated by the 105th TAS/118th AW of the Tennessee Air National Guard. This Nashville-based Hercules is one of the earliest to be found and has the original flat nose. It is at Greenham Common, June 1979.

Above: Despite being camouflaged this **C130E** 70-1274 of the 39th TAS/317th TAW Military Airlift Command shines in the sun and shows full colour markings, a far cry from the grey of today. It is seen at Lakenheath, August 1975.

Below: Fighting forest fires by water bombing is mainly a civil task in the USA with a number of specialised companies operating a range of permanently converted aircraft at high-risk locations during the summer months. The MAFFS (Modular Airborne Fire Fighting System) was developed in California. This can quickly be fitted into a C130 and can dispense 3000 US gallons of either water or retardant. **C130H** 93-7313 of the 302nd AW (Air Force Reserve Command) with the rear doors open and the MAFFS system showing is pictured at Fairford, July 1999.

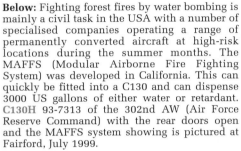

Below: Spain operates the C130 in both a transport and an air-refuelling role. Seen here, in a camouflage suitable for a semi-arid countryside, is **C130H** T.10.04 31-04 of Ala 31 based at Zaragoza. It was photographed at Fairford in July 1995.

Above: Operated by only one squadron, 356 Mira/112 Pterix at Elefsis the Greek Air Force has both C130B and H models in service. **C130H** 741 is seen on approach to Athens, June 1993.

Left: Configured as a flight-refuelling tanker Argentine Air Force **KC130H** TC-70 of 1 Brigade Aerea is pictured at Greenham Common, June 1981. Within twelve months this aircraft was supporting attack missions against the Royal Navy in the Falklands War.

Below: Seen here in an all-over light-grey colour scheme is C130H M30.07 from 4 Squadron of the Royal Malaysian Air Force. It is seen departing Fairford, July 1996.

Above: Only in the last few years has the Royal Netherlands Air Force obtained C130s. Prior to this the transport fleet consisted of F27s. C130H-30 G-273 is one of the two operated by the air arm. All the Dutch transports are operated by 334 Squadron at Eindhoven. Photographed at Fairford, July 1996.

Below: Based at Lod the Israeli Air Force operates both tanker and transport C130s. Their most famous operation was the raid in 1976 at Entebbe, Uganda to rescue the passengers from a highjacked Airbus. 436/4X-FWB is seen departing Greenham Common, June 1979.

Above: An operator of the Hercules since 1964 the Turkish Air Force has been one of the few air arms to keep them in a bare-metal finish. C130E 13186 12-186 of 222 Filo, based at Kayseri-Erkilet, is seen at Fairford, July 1995.

Left: Seen here with seventy-fifth anniversary markings is a 28 Squadron C130B of the South African Air Force. Based at Waterkloof the unit has operated the type since 1963. The original seven, all still in service, have been supplemented with ex-USAF airframes. 401 is at Fairford, July 1996.

Below: Seen on the ramp at Andrews AFB, Washington DC, May 1989 is C130H CH02 of the Belgian Air Force. All the Hercules fleet are operated by 20 SME at Melsbroek.

Right: The Royal Jordanian Air Force has been a C130 operator for over thirty years. They are all operated by 3 Squadron which has the nickname 'Guts Airline'. C130H 345 is at Fairford, July 1997. Its home base is Al Matar airbase, Amman.

Right: The first of the RAF's sixty-six C130Ks, known as Hercules C.Mk1s, were delivered at the end of 1966. Thirty of the fleet have been stretched by 15 ft (4.5 m) by Marshalls of Cambridge, these are designated C.Mk3. All the fleet is based at Lyneham and although there are five squadrons including the conversion unit, individual aircraft are not marked as such. **Hercules C1.P XV179** is seen landing at Finningley, September 1984. (The 'P' indicates it is equipped for in-flight refuelling.)

Below: Thailand is one of the countries using the stretched fuselage **C130H-30**. 60105 of 601 Squadron, Royal Thai Air Force, is at Phuket, November 1989. This unit is based at the capital, Bangkok.

Below: Australia has had three batches of Hercules deliveries: C130As in 1958, 'E's in 1966 and 'H' models in 1978. A97.160 is a **C130E** operated by RAAF 37 Squadron in a smart grey and white scheme. It is at Fairford, July 1994.

Above: Chile bought two new C130Hs in the early 1970s and added four ex-USAF C130Bs in the early 1990s. 996, one of the original **C130Hs** of 10 *Grupo*, based at Los Cerrillos, Santiago is at Fairford, July 1994.

Below: Italian Air Force C130s are no longer in full colour markings; camouflage has now taken over. **C130H** MM62001 46-15 of 46 *Brigate Aerea*, based at Pisa, is pictured at Cottesmore, June 1987 in the old high-visibility marks.

Below: There are two versions of the HC130H, one for the USAF and the other for the US Coast Guard. As well as its traditional role the type can carry an under wing pod with FLIR (Forward Looking Infra Red), an optical data link and a control console. This is used for anti-drug operations. **HC130H** 1704 of USCG Sacramento, CA is seen landing at Chico, September 1988. The USCG colour scheme is one of the smartest on any aircraft.

Below: The **DC130** is a drone director aircraft. It has the ability to carry four reconnaissance or target drones under the wings as well as the precision guidance equipment in the fuselage. Pictured at Mojave, CA, September 1988 is 560514 of the US Navy. (This is an ex-USAF airframe that carries its old air force serial in a navy style.) It is operated on their behalf by Flight Systems.

Left: The latest variant for the Hercules is the C130J. This is a completely new aircraft with glass cockpits and different powerplants. **Hercules C4** ZH873 shows off its new shape at Fairford, July 1999.

Below: Perhaps the oddest-looking C130 is the one operated by the Defence Evaluation and Research Agency's Meteorological Research Flight at Boscombe Down. To accommodate the 18 ft (5.49 m) long instrumentation boom the nose radar has been fitted onto the cockpit roof. **Hercules W2** XV208 is seen at Leuchars, September 1975.

Below: The US Navy purchased six ski-equipped **LC130R** aircraft for use in the various US bases in the Antarctica including the South Pole. 160741 01/XD of VXE6 'Puckered Penguins' is at London, Ont, June 1990. The squadron is based at Point Magu in sunny California.

Below: Used as a straight cargo carrier, the **C130F** is operated by the US Navy in small numbers. 149797 797/JM of VR24 is seen departing Greenham Common, June 1979.

Above: Following basic C130 flying, crews from the US Marine Corps join VMGRT 253. This squadron, based at Cherry Point, NC, then trains personnel for Marine operations and airborne tanking. **KC130F** 148249 249/GR of the unit is at Fairford, July 1994.

Above: Since the 'Blue Angels' is a navy unit (with some marine pilots) the USMC is tasked with the support role and has traditionally painted the aircraft accordingly. **C130F** 149806 is at Biggs AAF, TX, October 1984.

Below: The role of US Navy squadron VQ4 is known as TACAMO (Take Charge and Move Out). This involves communications with the fleet of ballistic missile submarines. The aircraft will trail a very long aerial and transmit in very low frequency. **EC130Q** 162312 of VX4 is at Patuxent River, MD, May 1989.

Above: Showing its stretch is **L100-30** FAE 893 of Ecuadorian Air Force unit Ala 11. It is at its base, Quito, September 1997.

Right: Portugal has one squadron of Hercules transports. This is Esq 501 based at Montijo. C130H 6803 is at Fairford, July 1989.

Below: Keeping the national markings low key is this Honduran Air Force machine. C130A FAH 559 is at Miami, June 1989.

Below: Unlike many countries the Colombian Air Force has some of its C130s in a full colour scheme. C130H FAC 1005 of Esc 711 is at its Bogotá base, September 1997.

Above: In the Venezuelan Air Force the C130s all have serials in no apparent order. This is common amongst other types as well. C130H 2716 is at Caracas, November 1992.

Below: The L100-30s of the Kuwait Air Force are adopting full colour markings. The fleet comes under the control of 41 Squadron based at Ali Salim Sabah air base. KAF 324 is at Fairford, July 1993.

Above: New Zealand had the first production C130Hs and has the 'J' model on order. Showing off its smart national markings is C130H NZ7002 of 40 Squadron RNZAF. It is seen flying at Finningley, June 1977.

Below: The civil registration on this Gabonese Air Force L100-30 does not hide its military use. TR-KKB is at Paris, June 1977.

Left: Clad in the usual dark colours of the type is **C130H** 954 of 335 Skv, Norwegian Air Force. The fleet of six is based at Oslo/Gardermoen. It was photographed at Fairford in July 1989.

Below: **C130A** TAM 66 of the Bolivian Air Force is operated in its original USAF colours with the national insignia changed. Operated by *Grupo Aereo* 71/Esc 711 from the capital La Paz, it is seen at Santa Cruz, November 1992.

Above: This Saudi **KC130H** tanker is in two-tone desert-sand colours. 3202 is operated by 32 Squadron and is seen at Fairford, July 1995.

Above: The Royal Saudi Air Force operates C130s in a number of roles aside from cargo; they have aircraft configured as VIP transports and as surgical operating theatres. **C130H** 1609 of 16 Squadron is in basic cargo mode. It was photographed at Greenham Common in June 1981.

Above: Canada started Hercules operations in 1960 and has upgraded to newer models several times. **CC130E** 130316 of 435 Squadron, based at Winnipeg, is seen in the well-known white/silver colours at Greenham Common, June 1979.

Above: The urge to paint over all the markings has caught up with the Canadians. **CC130E** 130307 of 435 Squadron is seen, in camouflage, at its Winnipeg base, June 1990.

Above: The transport unit of the Peruvian Air Force, *Grupo* 8, based at Lima, operates a mix of C130 models. **L100-20** FAP397/OB1375 has full colour markings. It is on the ramp at its base, September 1997.

Right: Algeria's stretched Hercules have retained their civil style markings. **C130H-30** 7T-WHA of the Algerian Air Force is pictured at Moscow, August 1995. (JDS)

Right: The Romanian Air Force was the first of the former Warsaw Pact countries to obtain the Hercules. **C130B** 5930 of 19 FMT was seen at its base, Bucharest/Otopeni in May 1999. The airframes are all ex-USAF machines. (PJD)

Below: The Blackburn Beverley started life as the General Aircraft GAL 60 Universal. Blackburn took over the company and first flew the big box-like freighter from Brough in June 1950. Powered by four Bristol Centaurus radial air-cooled piston engines it entered RAF service as the **Beverley C1**. Forty-seven production aircraft were built and the type left squadron service at the end of 1967. XB287/T of 47 Squadron, based at Abingdon, was photographed at Lakenheath in May 1965. (AG)

Above: Derived from the Antonov An-14 the An-28 was deemed to be such an upgrade as to get a new number. Production was not in Russia but in Poland by PZL. A twin turboprop high-wing transport it can carry seventeen passengers or a 2000 kg payload. **PZL Mielec An-28** (NATO code-name Cash) 1003 of 13 PLT Polish Air Force is at its Kraków/Balice base, April 1998. (PJD)

Left: Acquired as a troop transport the Vickers (now BAe) VC10 joined 10 Squadron RAF in 1966. In 1992 following the Gulf War the decision was taken to convert these to C1.Ks to give the unit a dual tanker/transport role. **VC10 C1.K** XV102 is seen on approach to Manchester–Ringway, June 1996 in the original fleet colours.

Above: A number of ex-British, Gulf and East African Airways VC10s were purchased by the RAF for conversion to pure tanker roles. **VC10 K2** ZA140/A of 101 Squadron is seen departing from Fairford, July 1995 in the tanker's hemp colour scheme.

Above: Code-named Coaler by NATO, the **Antonov An-72** was developed to replace the An-26. It is a high-wing transport powered by two ZMDB Progress D36 turbofans. 949(Black) of the Soviet Air Force is seen on a rare visit to the UK. It is at Scampton, July 1991.

Left: Seen here in Ukrainian Air Force markings is 07(Red), an Antonov An-72P. This variant is a dedicated maritime patrol aircraft, as well as this it is armed with 23 mm cannon and rocket pods. It was photographed at Farnborough in September 1992.

Below: Outside its native Ukraine, and of course Russia, the only other military user of the Antonov An-72 is Peru. *Grupo* 8 at Lima operates these. OB-1485 only wore a civil registration when pictured on the ramp at its base, September 1997.

Below: Spanish built, the CASA 212 has found a market in the light transport role. A high-wing twin turboprop, it has as well as the traditional tasks been converted to other specialist military versions. TE.12B-41 79-94 of Ala 72 of the Spanish Air Force is at Boscombe Down, June 1992.

Below: The Cessna U3A was a military variant of the popular 310A twin-engined 5/6-seat private aircraft. Its use was in an unarmed liaison role. 57-5918 U3A of the Wisconsin National Guard was photographed at the state capital, Madison, in August 1974. (SGW)

Left: As well as the illustrated transport role the Portuguese Air Force operates a pair of CASA 212s equipped for electronic warfare. 16512 of Esq 401 was seen at its base, Sintra, in March 1997. (PJD)

Above: Once a familiar sight, day-glo has all but disappeared from the military palette of colours. Seen at Opa Locka, FL, in August 1986, prior to delivery is CASA 212 MP-313 of the Mexican Navy. The eleven aircraft in the fleet are split amongst five bases.

Left: The 300-series CASA 212 can be spotted by winglets and a longer nose. Seen at Medellín, November 1992 is CASA 212-300 FAC 1158 of the Colombian Air Force airline SATENA. This operation by military aircraft and aircrew is to provide services to and from locations that may not be economical for a civilian operator.

Right: The Irish Air Corps uses its CN 235s for coastal patrol work. CN 235MPA 252 of the Maritime Squadron is seen at Fairford, July 1998.

Below: CN 235M-100 ANE 202 is operated as a transport aircraft by Esq 2 of the Ecuadorian Navy. It is seen at the Navy's sole base, Guayaquil, September 1997.

Below: Unlike the white colours of the navy the Ecuadorian Army has all its aircraft in camouflage. CN 235M AEE 502 is operated by *Grupo Aereo* 43. It is seen at Quito, September 1997.

Below: Assembled in Turkey by TAI the Turkish Air Force has used CN 235s to replace Dakotas. 051 is operated by 223 *Filo*. It is pictured at its base, Etimesgut, May 1998. (PJD)

Above: Such was the success of the CASA 212 that the company got together with the Indonesian manufacturer IPTN to develop a larger variant for both civil and military use. Sales have been very good with twenty-one different air arms operating the new aircraft. Airtech (CASA/IPTN) CN 235 CNA-MB of Transport Aviation Command of the Moroccan Air Force is pictured at Fairford, July 1995. The unit's home base is Kenitra.

Above: Military Fokker F28 Fellowships are usually found in single numbers providing VIP transports to presidents and prime ministers. F28-1000 FAC 0001 is the Colombian Air Force presidential aircraft. It is seen on the ramp at Bogotá, under guard, September 1997.

Left: The Beech 18 light transport and trainer has had a very long life from its first flight in 1937. The production line ran until 1969 when the last variant was built. 134713 SNB-5 (C45) was one of a batch of twenty supplied to the French Navy. It was seen at Tousous in June 1967. (SGW)

Above: Purchased by the USAF for the distribution of aircraft spare parts around its European bases the C23A Sherpa was a cargo variant of the Short 330 commuter liner. They were later passed to the US Army for general cargo operations. C23B 93-1333 of Co.D 1-207th AVN Alaska NG is seen at its Fort Richardson base, May 2000.

Below: A number of different manufacturers, including Beech, offered conversions of the Beech 18 to nose wheel configuration. FAC 5579 is such a conversion. Operated by the Colombian Air Force it is seen at Madrid AFB, September 1997.

Above: The de Havilland Comet was the first jet airliner in service in the world. RAF Transport Command purchased ten Comet C2s in 1956. They were used as troop transports by 216 Squadron, the first military jet transport squadron in the world. The last Comet used was XS235, a 4C; it was operated for test work by the A&AEE and is seen flying at Fairford, July 1994.

Below: Like the C130 the An-12 has had many more roles than just transport. This example 43(Red) is an An-12BP (Mod) of the Russian Air Force. It is used to test ejector seats, these can be fired either up or down from the cone in the tail. On the wing tips are cameras to record the events. It is pictured at its Zhukovsky base, August 1997. (JDS)

Above: When the GDR (East Germany) was rejoined with the rest of the nation the two air forces merged. The *Luftwaffe* found they had a variety of types they did not want. Some were never taken into service whilst others were operated for a few years and sold on. Such an example was the Tupolev Tu-154M jet liner. 11+01 is seen at Boscombe Down, June 1992.

Above: The Warsaw Pact countries operated the Antonov An-12 in the same roles as the west did with the C130. Both aircraft have the same general layout of high wings, four turboprops and rear ramp loading. The An-12 had been developed from the earlier twin-engined An-8. An-12BP 2105 of 1 SDLP of the Czechoslovakian Air Force is at Boscombe Down, June 1992.

Below: Other former Warsaw Pact nations still operated the Tu-154, as this tri jet is cheap and reliable. Many can be found in airline service especially in the former Soviet Republics. Tu-154M 101 of 36 SPLT, Polish Air Force, is seen at its base Warsaw/Okecie, April 1998. (PJD)

Left: Following the peaceful split of Czechoslovakia into the Czech Republic and Slovakia most of the air force was divided on a 2:1 basis to the Czechs. They also kept the old national markings. Tu-154B2 0601 of 61 DTL is at its Prague/Kbely base, August 1998. (PJD)

Right: Finland operates **Piper PA28 Cherokee Arrows** for light transport and liaison duties. PA-11 is seen at the Air Support Command HQ, Tikkakoski, June 1998.

Above: Showing that the **C5A** can be loaded from the front as well as the rear is 70-0466 of the 436th MAW at Tyndall AFB, FL, April 1994. It also shows the current overall grey paint of the fleet.

Above: The **Lockheed C5A Galaxy** is well known for its vast size. It is a four-engined high-wing strategic transport with a capacity for up to 350 troops or 265,000 lb of cargo. 69-0019 of the 436th MAW departs Greenham Common in the original white and grey colours, June 1981.

Below: The Cessna O-2A was a full military version of the 337 Super Skymaster. It had underwing hard points and clear panels in the lower part of the door for extra visibility. The main use was that of a forward air controller. **Cessna O-2A** 69-7667 is at Harlingen, TX, October 1979.

Above: **Short's SC7 Skyvan** is an ideal light transport capable of carrying bulky cargo or for other uses such as parachute training from its rear opening doors. 5S-TB Skyvan 3M is operated by 3 Wing, Austrian Air Force. It was photographed at Greenham Common in July 1976.

Above: Built by Hunting Percival, the Pembroke entered RAF service during 1953 as an Anson replacement. One version was used in a photo reconnaissance role. **Pembroke C1** XL953 of 60 Squadron is at Wildenrath, June 1978.

Below: **Fairchild's C123 Provider** was a twin piston-engined variant of the Chase C20 glider. The C123 had a rough field performance and was heavily involved in the Vietnam War. To give extra power some were converted to have a pair of 2850 lb thrust J85 jets under the wings, these were known as C123Ks. **C123K** 54-0580 of the US Air Force Reserve is at Harlingen, TX, October 1979.

Below: Three years before the RAF had the Pembroke the Royal Navy had received the first Sea Prince. The role of the type was as a light transport; later versions were used as navigation trainers. **Sea Prince C1** WF138 907/BY is an early short-nosed variant. It is operated as the station hack at RNAS Brawdy where it was photographed in July 1963. (AG)

Left: With a high-wing, twin-boom and twin piston engines the **Nord 2501 Noratlas** was a French-built transport. Deliveries commenced in 1953 and as well as the French Air Force aircraft were sold to Israel, Greece, Portugal, Niger and West Germany among others. GC+115 is a *Luftwaffe*-operated aircraft with a mix of camouflage and day-glo in its colour scheme. It is pictured at Odiham, September 1964. (AG)

Below: As well as transport the bulky airframe of the **Noratlas** meant it could be used for various test work. No. 29 is operated by the CEV (*Centre D'essais en Vol*), a research establishment. It is seen at Châteaudun, June 1977 with non-standard wing tips.

Above: The Yakovlev **Yak-40** (NATO name Codling) has proved to be a success as a feeder airliner as well as a military transport; in this latter role it is usually as a VIP transport. 71503 of the Yugoslavian Air Force is at Paris–Orly, June 1977.

Above: The **Piper PA34 Seneca** is a popular six-seat twin-engined aircraft used in the private and business market place, and over 2500 have been built. They are also used by the military as light communications aircraft. FAC 5200 is operated by the Colombian Air Force and is seen at Madrid AFB, September 1997. Some of the PA34s operated by the Colombian military are impounded drug runners that they regard as 'free' aircraft for their use.

Left: The first aeroplane to enter production in Germany following World War II was the Dornier Do27, a STOL utility and liaison aircraft. It was actually designed in Spain so it is of small wonder that it was built there under licence as the **CASA 127**. U.9.32 of Spanish Air Force unit Ala 23 is seen at Talavera La Real, March 1997. (PJD)

Below: This Polish Air Force **Yak-40**, 037, was seen attending a European summit meeting about Bosnia being held at Athens in June 1993.

Below: Bolivia's air force is another user of the **PA34 Seneca** in the utility role. FAB 208 is at Santa Cruz, November 1992.

Below: The overall grey, lack of windows and extra aerials indicate a different role for this US Army **RC12D**, 80-23375 of the 1st MIB (Military Intelligence Battalion). Its task is to intercept and analyse enemy radio signals. It is seen at Mildenhall, May 1985.

Right: This US Army **U21A** is operated by the US Navy Test Pilots School at Patuxent River, MD. 67-18096 is seen at its base, May 1989.

Above: Used by the British Army Air Corps, the **Auster AOP9** was a 2/3-seat air observation post and light liaison aircraft. First flown in 1954 it was powered by a single 185 hp Bombardier liquid cooled piston engine. XR243 is seen at Valley, August 1968. (SGW)

Above: The standard US military liaison aircraft is the **Beech C12**. Based upon the successful Beechcraft King Air series they perform a multitude of functions. **C12A** 76-0168 is a USAF machine serving as an embassy flight aircraft. It is seen at Bogotá, Colombia, September 1997.

Below: Cessna's 400 range of 6/9-seater light transports are used by commuter air taxi companies and by military units for liaison work. **Cessna 402C** AB-102 is operated by the Bolivian Navy. A quick glance at a map will show that Bolivia is a land-locked country. However it does have Lake Titicaca, an area of 3200 square miles so can boast a naval unit. It is seen at its La Paz base, November 1992.

Below: The **Beech T44 Pegasus** is used by the US Navy as a multi-engine pilot trainer for aircrews destined for the P3 Orion and other such types. 161067/D of Training Wing 4 based at Corpus Christi, TX is pictured on a visit to Pensacola, FL, October 1981.

Above: **Beech King Air F90** FAB 018 is used by the Bolivian Air Force as a VIP transport. Operated by Esc 311 it is seen at its base, La Paz, November 1992.

Below: Showing its almost standard civil colour scheme is **Beech King Air 300** AN-232 operated by Esc 2 of the Ecuadorian Navy. It is seen on a visit to Quito, September 1997.

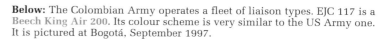

Below: The Colombian Army operates a fleet of liaison types. EJC 117 is a **Beech King Air 200**. Its colour scheme is very similar to the US Army one. It is pictured at Bogotá, September 1997.

Above: The **C12J** is the US military designation of the Beech 1900 commuter airliner. The C12 number is still used for what is a very different-looking type. 86-0079 of the US Army HQ USECOM is at Fairford, July 1999.

Below: The military variant of the Douglas DC4 Skymaster was the C54. It was used by the USAF in large numbers as a general transport aircraft. **C54E** 44-9100 is at Upper Heyford, June 1969. (SGW)

Above: France operates this ex-Jordanian Airlines Airbus **A310-304** in a VIP role. F-RADB/422 is at Paris–Le Bourget, June 1999. (SGW)

Above: The rough field performance of the **G222** makes it a useful transport for some of the remote parts of Thailand. Operated by 603 Squadron, Royal Thai Air Force, 60310 is seen at its Bangkok base, November 1999.

Below: In 1955 Convair converted thirty-eight Douglas C54 Skymasters to the role of search aircraft for the USAF Air Rescue Service. **SC54D** 42-72696 is seen at its Prestwick base in May 1963. In those days the use of day-glo was widespread. (AG)

Above: The first of the Airbus range to find service in military colours was the A310. **A310-304** 15002 is operated by 437 Squadron, Canadian Armed Forces, from its base at Trenton, Ont. It is known in service as the **CC150 Polaris**. It is pictured at Liverpool–Speke, May 1993.

Below: The **Alenia (Aeritalia/Fiat) G222** is a twin-turboprop high-wing transport. A variant was acquired by the USAF as the C27A Spartan. MM62128 RS-48 of the Italian Air Force RSV (Test Unit) is at Fairford, July 1989.

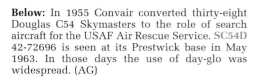

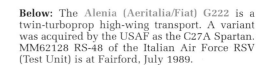

Right: With a long held reputation for building practical workhorse-like aeroplanes de Havilland (Canada) aircraft are renowned for their short field performance. One such design is the DHC6 Twin Otter. With a high-wing, twin turboprops and a fixed undercarriage it has found favour in many air arms. No. 745/CV is a French Air Force example operated by ET65, a medium-weight aircraft transport unit. It is pictured at Conningsby, June 1989.

Below: The Ilyushin IL-14 (NATO code-name Crate) was the main medium transport aircraft during the 1950s with the then Soviet Union and its satellite states. Later roles included navigation training and electronic intelligence. 06(Blue) of the Russian Air Force is at Tushino, Moscow, August 1995.

Below: Many parts of Ecuador are remote and have very basic airstrips. This DHC6 Twin Otter, FAE 451 from Esc 1111, is at the unit's base, Quito, September 1997. Note the large low-pressure tyres for rough locations.

Above: This Canadian Armed Forces DHC6 Twin Otter is a 100 series, note the shorter nose. 440 Squadron from Yellow Knife in the North West Territories of the country operates it. CC138 Twin Otter 13804 is at its base, May 2000.

Below: As the only purpose-built water bomber the Canadair CL215 is used mainly by the various provincial governments in Canada to fight forest fires. They have also been sold to a number of Mediterranean countries to contain fires during their hot dry summers. As a seaplane it can skim lakes or other large areas of water and through scoops under the fuselage fill its tanks with water. This can be dropped on to a fire either in one big drop or several smaller ones using the different sets of tank doors. Here, 1039 of Greek Air Force unit 355 Mira lands at Athens, June 1993. This squadron is based at Elefsis.

Above: With a production run of just nineteen complete aircraft including prototypes the VFW-Fokker 614 was never going to be an important civil or military type. It was a medium-range passenger transport aircraft. The most notable feature was that the engines were mounted on pylons above the wings. The only military user was the *Luftwaffe*. 17+02 is seen landing at Manchester–Ringway, May 1993.

Below: The Douglas C124 Globemaster II was a heavy cargo transport. Powered by four 3800 hp P&W R4360 radial piston engines it would load its payload through a set of doors under the nose. C124A 51-0178 is at Pittsburgh, August 1970 on charge to the AFRes. (SGW)

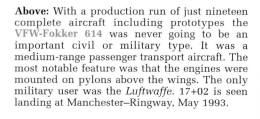

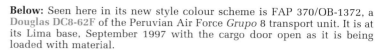

Below: Seen here in its new style colour scheme is FAP 370/OB-1372, a Douglas DC8-62F of the Peruvian Air Force *Grupo* 8 transport unit. It is at its Lima base, September 1997 with the cargo door open as it is being loaded with material.

Above: When the latest transport came from McDonnell Douglas, the C17, it was given the name **Globemaster III**. This four-engined high-wing cargo aircraft has state-of-the-art operational equipment to give STOL performance from unprepared airfields. 94-0065 of the 437th AW is seen on a refuelling stop at Elmendorf AFB, Alaska, May 2000.

Below: The Douglas DC8 has never achieved in military service what its rival the Boeing 707 has, however more DC8s can be found as cargo aircraft compared to the 707s due to the Douglas company stretching the airframe and fitting new generation engines. **Douglas DC8-62CF** FAP 371 of *Grupo* 8, Peruvian Air Force, is seen at Miami, August 1986.

Above: The **Fairchild C119 Flying Boxcar** was a logical development from the company's earlier C82 Packet. It was a twin-boom tactical transport loaded from rear cargo doors. It was later used as a gun ship. CP35 is a Belgian Air Force **C119G** of 15 Wing. It is at North Weald, May 1972.

Below: One of the most low-profile users of the Dash 7 is the US Army. Under a programme called 'Airborne Reconnaissance Low' it operates a small number of the type with civil registrations and small US Army titles under the cockpit. **EO-5B (DHC7)** N705GG of 204th MIB is at Gomez AFB, Colombia, September 1997. Locations such as this are visited in connection with anti-drug operations.

Above: Following the company trend of STOL aircraft de Havilland (Canada) produced the **DHC7 Dash 7**. This was a four-engined fifty-seat aircraft. It was used for some years by the Canadian Armed Forces under the designation **CC132**. 132001 of 412 Squadron arrived at Fairford in July 1985 in what was then a standard colour scheme for Canadian transport aircraft.

Left: The US Marine Corps was a major operator of the C119; originally designated R4Q-2s they became C119Fs in 1962 following the unified service designations. The variant differed from the R4Q-1 as it had two Wright 3400 hp radial piston engines in place of the Pratt & Whitney R43260s of the earlier model. **C119F** 131677/QH is operated by USMC transport squadron VMR 234. It is pictured at Glenview NAS, August 1974. (SGW)

Right: The Short SC5 Belfast was a long-range strategic freighter with a large bulk capacity. Operated by only one unit, 53 Squadron, they had entered service by the end of 1966. Defence cuts had the type out of service ten years later. They were sold on the civil market and were leased by the RAF for the Falklands War as they needed the type's load capacity. Belfast C1 XR371 is at Leuchars, September 1974. This was the last aircraft built.

Below: First flown in 1956 the Douglas C133 Cargomaster was a heavy-lift strategic freighter built for the USAF Military Air Transport Service. Cargo was loaded via rear freight doors. The type left service during the early 1970s. C133A 56-2011 of the 436th MAW is at Lakenheath, June 1970. (SGW)

Below: Lockheed's C141 Starlifter was a great leap in performance of cargo aircraft when it entered service with the USAF in 1964. NC141A 61-2776 of the 4950th TW Air Force Systems Command is at London, Ont, June 1990 in the colour scheme first used by the type.

Above: In 1977 the first C141B flew. This was a 23 ft stretch together with air-to-air refuelling capability. All but one of the surviving C141A airframes were converted to C141B level. 64-0612 in its all-over camouflage is at Hamilton, Ont, June 1990.

Below: The Tupolev Tu-134 (NATO code-name Crusty) is a twin-engined medium-range airliner. They are used for transport and VIP roles. Tu-134 1407 of 1 Transport Regiment, Czechoslovakian Air Force, is at Fairford, July 1991.

Below: Bulgarian Air Force aircraft were very rare visitors to the UK. Tu-134A LZ.D.050 of 16 TAB, based at Vrazhdebna, is seen at Fairford, July 1995.

Below: As a follow on to the DC4 the Douglas company produced the DC6; this had the same basic layout but was longer, had pressurisation and more powerful engines. The military version had a cargo floor and door. C118B 131578, US Navy Keflavik, was at Mildenhall in June 1984 near the end of the type's service life.

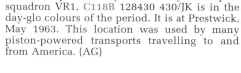

Below: Operated by US Navy transport squadron VR1, **C118B** 128430 430/JK is in the day-glo colours of the period. It is at Prestwick, May 1963. This location was used by many piston-powered transports travelling to and from America. (AG)

Above: The latest aircraft from Dornier is the stylish Do328. Currently the only military user is the Colombian Air Force airline SATENA. **Do328-100** FAC 1160 is at Bogotá, September 1997.

Below: After being seized for an alleged drug offence this **Douglas DC6** was put into service by the Peruvian Air Force. FAP 381 is at Lima, September 1997.

Below: Royal Moroccan Air Force **Dornier Do28** CNA-NP/4336 is pictured in desert camouflage at Fairford, July 1989. They are used as maritime patrol aircraft from their base at Rabat-Salé.

Below: The Belgian Air Force purchased this **Douglas DC6A** from the national airline SABENA, operating it from 1960 to 1977 when it was sold. OT-CDF/KY4 is at Odiham, September 1964. (AG)

Below: The **Dornier Do28D Skyservant** is a simple light transport, freighter and liaison aircraft. It has a high-wing and its two piston engines are mounted on stub wings. The undercarriage is fixed. 58+97 of the *Luftwaffe* is at Paris, June 1977.

Below: Following on from the Do28 the Dornier company produced the **Do228**. This was a longer turboprop aircraft performing many of the earlier types roles. 57+02 is operated by German Navy unit MFG3. Based at Nordholz they are used both as transports and as pollution control aircraft. 57+02 is pictured at Fairford, July 1999.

Above: The North American/Rockwell Sabreliner business jet was bought 'off the shelf' by the US military. Its uses varied from training to VIP transport. **VT39** 61-0685 of the USAF is at Leuchars, September 1976.

Right: The military version of the Boeing Stratocruiser was the C97. It had many common parts to the B29 bomber including the wing, tail and powerplants. These were four P&W R4360s of 3500 hp each. **VC97K** 52-2730 of HQ 16th Air Force Torrejon is at Liverpool–Speke, May 1968. In passenger configuration, it was transporting a military band.

Above: Used by the US Navy for training navigators the **T39A** has been in service since 1963. 150985 600/F of Training Wing 6 is at its Pensacola base, October 1981.

Above: FAE 043 **Sabreliner 40R** of *Escuadron Presidencial*, Ecuadorian Air Force is fitted out for VIP transport work. It is at its Quito base, September 1997.

Below: The most common use of the C97 was as a flying tanker to support the SAC fleet of B47s. These were later passed on to ANG units who operated the type until the mid-1970s. **KC97L** 52-0905 of 126th ARS Wisconsin ANG takes off from Greenham Common, July 1973. The home base for this unit was Milwaukee.

Above: This **T39D** has an extended nose. It is operated by the US Navy Test Pilots School. 150987 39/ is at its Patuxent River, MD base, May 1989.

Below: **KC97L** 52-2630 is operated by the 145th ARS Ohio ANG. The 'L' variant had extra power from two J47 jets mounted under the wings. It is pictured at Greenham Common, July 1974. The unit's home base was Rickenbacker AFB.

Below: An 'off-the-shelf' purchase of the Douglas DC9 for an aeromedical evacuation aircraft resulted in the **C9A Nightingale**. All the aircraft carry the red cross on the fin. 71-0881 of the 322nd TAW USAF is at Greenham Common, July 1973.

Left: Seen here in the stylish VVIP markings associated with the unit is 73-1683 **VC9C** of the 89th MAW based at Andrews AFB. It is pictured at New York–La Guardia, May 1989.

Below: The Convair 540 was built in Canada as the CL66A, this variant was powered by Napier Eland turboprops. Following the Rolls-Royce take-over of Napier the Eland was cancelled and eventually the aircraft were re-engined with Allisons to become Convair 580s. **CC109** 109157 of the Canadian Armed Forces is at Montreal, August 1974. (SGW)

Above: Ordered first as a navigation trainer and then as a transport the T29 was based upon the civil Convair 240. **T29B** 51-7892 is operated by 513rd TAW at Mildenhall as a general hack. It is pictured at Bentwaters, May 1972.

Above: US Navy operations have used C9s in both passenger and cargo roles. **C9B** 162391/RT of VR60 is at Andrews AFB, May 1989.

Above: **C131F** 141023 of NAS Mildenhall is pictured at its base, August 1978. This variant is the same as the civil Convair 340.

Above: The US Coast Guard used Convairs for a number of years in the coastal patrol role. **HC131A** 5799 of USCG Miami is pictured at its Opa Locka base, October 1981. This station is one of the most active in the service as it is on the front-line in the war against drugs coming in from South America.

Above: The type that the C9 replaced in the medical evacuation role was the **MC131**. This was one of the variants of the Convair range of airliners. 52-5787 of 439th MAG USAF is at Liverpool–Speke collecting personnel from the US Army base at Burtonwood, June 1968.

Right: This turboprop **Convair 580** was purchased from a civil operator by the Bolivian Air Force and operated as a general passenger/cargo aircraft. TAM 70 is on charge to Esc 712, based at La Paz, and is seen on the ramp at Santa Cruz, November 1992.

Below: The largest aeroplane in the Colombian Army is **Convair 580** EJC 121. An ex-civil aircraft it is used in a passenger/cargo role. It is pictured at its Bogotá base, September 1997.

Above: The early 1950s saw the birth of what we now know as AWACs. The US Navy were fitting various radar sets above and below the fuselages of Lockheed Constellations. The idea was picked up by the USAF who operated their own. **EC121T** 54-2307 of the 20th ADS is at Mildenhall near the end of the service life of the type, August 1978.

Above: Over half the production of the de Havilland (Canada) DHC2 Beaver went to the US military. The US Army was the largest user of this STOL light transport. It could operate from rough fields or even with skis or on floats. **U6A** 56-60387 of the US Army is at Heidelburg, West Germany, July 1970. It has a gloss-green finish and full-colour national markings.

Above: Before operating the much modified 'Rivet Rider' C130s the 193rd TEWS (Tactical Electronic Warfare Squadron), as they were then known, of the Pennsylvania ANG flew Lockheed Constellations. **C121C** 54-0157 is at Greenham Common, July 1974.

Above: The main use by the USAF for the Beaver was that of a station or squadron hack. In bare metal and day-glo **U6A** 53-8170 'LG-170' is operated by the Wethersfield-based 20th TFW. It is pictured at Ternhill, September 1963. This photograph is of note as it features one of the rare uses of the Beaver's 'LG' buzz code. (AG)

Above: The Royal Dutch Air Force had just nine **DHC2 Beavers**. They were delivered in November 1956 and used in the army co-operation role. S8 is at Deelen, June 1973. This aircraft has a 316 Squadron badge on its fin. This unit was a NF5A/B unit at Gilze-Rijen indicating the Beaver's use as a hack.

Below: This Constellation is one of the shorter fuselage L749s. **C121A** 48-0612 of the 7101st Air Base Wing is used by the HQ USAFE for transporting staff around NATO stations from its base at Wiesbaden. It is pictured at Prestwick, July 1964. (AG)

Above: **U6A Beaver** 150191 of 31/USNTPS is used as a one-off training aircraft for test pilots. It is pictured at its Patuxent River, MD base, May 1989. It makes an ideal test machine as it is unlikely that any of the normal fast jet pilots going through TPS would have flown anything like a Beaver.

Below: Within the British armed forces only the Army Air Corps used the Beaver. The aircraft were built in Canada, crated and shipped to the de Havilland factory at Chester for assembly. Beaver AL1 XP772 is at Little Rissington, August 1964. (AG)

Above: The executive jet has proved to be popular with air forces worldwide. It can be used as a VIP transport for senior officers and heads of state or as a special role aircraft with electronic warfare systems fitted. Seen at London–Heathrow, April 1990 is Dassault Falcon 20 TM.11-3 of Torrejon-based Esc 408. This Spanish Air Force unit is part of the *Centro de Inteligencia Aerea*. (SGW)

Below: January 1977 saw the sale of forty-one Dassault Falcon 20s to the US Coast Guard. Designated HU25A Guardians they have many extra features to fit the over-water surveillance role. As well as this standard fit many are specially configured for such tasks as pollution monitoring and anti-drug operations. 2108 of USCG Miami is at its Opa Locka base, August 1986.

Below: Used by the French Navy for a host of tasks the Dassault Falcon 10MER is one of the smaller 'biz' jets on the market. No. 133 of 3S, based at Landivisiau, is at Fairford, July 1989.

Below: Norway's Air Force uses its Dassault Falcon 20s for both VIP and ECM roles. 0125 of 717 Skv is seen at Liverpool–Speke, August 1979.

Above: A small number of Piper PA31 Navajos are used by the Finnish Air Force for transport and communications. This is a 6/8-seater civil transport adapted for military use. PC-3 is at Tikkakoski, June 1998.

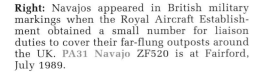

Right: Navajos appeared in British military markings when the Royal Aircraft Establishment obtained a small number for liaison duties to cover their far-flung outposts around the UK. PA31 Navajo ZF520 is at Fairford, July 1989.

Right: Now that Hungary is a member of NATO it is looking to upgrade equipment to western types. The first items are the 'sharp end' fast jets but the transports will no doubt follow. Antonov An-26 02204 is seen at Boscombe Down, June 1992.

Above: Designed to replace the IL-14 piston-engined transports the Antonov An-24 (NATO code-name Coke) had the same basic layout as a number of late 1950s turboprops, i.e. high wing and twin engines. It is used by a number of countries as a military transport. 2903 of LETKA 321 of the Slovak Air Force is at Fairford, July 1998.

Below: The logical development for the An-24 was to give it a rear loading ramp for easy loading of bulky cargo and having the ability to air drop it. This new aircraft was designated the Antonov An-26 (NATO code-name Curl). It was sold to many communist and third world states. 2507 is a Czech Air Force An-26 of 1 DVLP. It is at Mildenhall, May 1993. Note the rear ramp is down.

Above: Following the conflict over Kosovo, aircraft from the Federal Republic of Yugoslavia are unlikely to be seen outside that much-shrunken state. Antonov An-26 71385 is pictured at Hradec Králové in the Czech Republic, August 1998, before the armed clash with NATO. It was there to support aircraft from the national aerobatic team. (PJD)

Above: Antonov An-24 5803 of 61 DLT is operated by the Czech Air Force. It is seen at Fairford, July 1996.

Below: The French Navy found a replacement for the Flamant in the Navajo. They were used as unit hacks to ferry people and parts to the required locations. No. 916 of 3S is at Toussus-le-Nobel, May 1977.

Left: This Antonov An-26 of the Slovak Air Force is seen at Mildenhall, May 1996. Operated by 1 LETKA/32 ZmDk it is based at Piestany.

Below: Seen here in an all-over grey is Antonov An-26 1406 of Polish Air Force unit 13PLT. It is pictured at its Kraków/Balice base, April 1998. (PJD)

Above: When the two Germanys reunited the *Luftwaffe* found itself with a number of An-26s. These were only operated for a couple of years before being disposed of. 52+06 of TS24 is at Cottesmore, July 1991.

Left: The most powerful of the twin Antonov range is the An-32 (NATO code-name Cline). Its engines are mounted over the wing and are nearly twice the shaft horsepower of the An-24. It has an excellent 'hot and high' performance. FAP327 of *Grupo* 8, Peruvian Air Force, is on the ramp at its Lima base, September 1997. Note it has a very smart colour scheme; this particular aircraft is configured for passengers.

Above: Based upon the airframe of the An-24 the Antonov An-30 (NATO code-name Clank) is a dedicated survey and photographic platform. The clear-view nose is the recognition point. 04(Black) of the Russian Air Force is used for the 'Open Skies' policy of overflights. It is pictured at Fairford, July 1999.

Below: Another 'Open Skies' Antonov An-30 is this Czech Air Force example. Note it carries the titles for its role on the fin. It is operated by 344Dplet. It is seen at Fairford, July 1998.

Above: First flown in 1947, the French Dassault MD312 Flamant had three versions: transport, six-seat passenger or bombing and navigation trainer. No. 142 is seen in the passenger role at Odiham, September 1966. (AG)

Above: Developed by Armstrong Whitworth (then HS) the Argosy was a medium-range tactical transport for the RAF. Four Rolls-Royce Dart turboprops provided power. It was a twin-boom aircraft and the rear doors could be opened in flight for supply drops. Argosy C1 XN817 is at Coltishall, September 1971. It is operated by the A&AEE hence the non-standard colour scheme.

Below: Defence cuts curtailed the service life of the Argosy. The last unit to use the type were 115 Squadron; their role was to provide radar calibration duties from their base at Brize Norton. **Argosy E1** XN855 is at Abingdon, June 1977.

Above: Canadair's CL44 used the same wing, tail surfaces and undercarriage as the Britannia, the fuselage was however longer. The powerplants also differed being Rolls-Royce Tynes. Most commercial operators had the CL44D-4 with a swing tail for ease of loading cargo. The CL44-6 for the Royal Canadian Air Force lacked this feature and had cargo doors both front and rear on the port side. They were known in service as the Yukon. **CC106** 15922 is at London–Gatwick in August 1968.

Above: Entering service in 1948 the Handley Page Hastings had a long service life. Its role was as a long-range transport powered by four 1675 hp Bristol Hercules radial piston engines. **Hastings C1A** TG527 of 36 Squadron, RAF Transport Command, is at Odiham, September 1966. (AG)

Above: Introduced in 1959 the Bristol Britannia gave the RAF a long-range turboprop troop carrier to cover the world-wide bases then in operation. **Britannia C1** XM489 of 99 Squadron is at St Mawgan, August 1974. Defence cuts had the type out of service two years later.

Above: The **Antonov An-2** (NATO code-name Colt) has been built in larger numbers than any other post-war aircraft. It is a large, single-engined biplane able to carry up to fourteen passengers. It can be operated from rough strips, on skis, or floats; it is almost the perfect utility aircraft. 147 of the 3rd Transport Esk of the Latvian Air Force is seen at its base, Lielvarde, May 1995. Note the exotic markings on the fuselage. (JDS)

Above: Russia was naturally the main user of the **Antonov An-2**. One large user is DOSAAF; this translates as 'Voluntary Society for the Support of the Army, Aviation and Fleet'. It operates as a paramilitary organisation with its aircraft in military marks. Among its functions are flying and parachute training. 34(White) of DOSAAF is at Chaika, August 1991.

Right: The T5 model of the Hastings was developed to train bomb aimers. It had a large ventral radome under the fuselage containing the radar set. **Hastings T5** TG511 of 230 OCU/SCBS (Strike Command Bombing School) is at St Mawgan, July 1974.

Left: Like with so many types the A&AEE at Boscombe Down was the last user of the Hastings. **Hastings C1A** TG500 is at its base, March 1971. Note the extended nose and underwing tanks.

Below: The Finnish Air Force uses its three Learjets to perform a multitude of tasks. These include target towing, aerial mapping, electronic warfare training and maritime patrol. Learjet 35A LJ3 is pulled from its hangar with a target towing device under the wing. It is operated by the 1st Flight of the Air Support Squadron at Tikkakoski where it was photographed in June 1998.

Above: As with many business jets the Learjet has many functions in the air arms that it serves. This USAF example C21A Learjet 84-0113 is operated as a passenger aircraft by the 1402nd MAS and is seen at Andrews AFB, May 1989.

Below: Built in Brazil by Embraer, the EMB121 Xingu is a six-passenger, pressurised corporate turboprop. The powerplants are two P&W (Canada) PT6s. The French military are major users of the type. 52S (French Navy) operates the aircraft from its base at Lahn-Bihoue in the role of navigator trainers. No.79 is seen at Finningley, September 1991.

Below: The Pilatus PC6 Porter has been built with both piston and turboprop power. The aircraft is a single-engine, high-wing utility type with STOL performance. V-615, a turbo, of the Swiss Air Force is seen at Dübendorf, August 1987.

Below: The powerplants on the twin-engined Piaggio P166 are distinctive in that they act as pushers with the propellers being on the trailing edge of the wing. Italian-built, their role is communications between bases. A number are however configured for photo survey work and have vertical mounted cameras in the fuselage. Such an example is P166DL-3 MM25154 303-21 of 303 *Gruppo*. It is pictured at Cottesmore, June 1988.

Above: Conceived as a joint venture between Piaggio and Douglas the PD808 business jet failed to sell in the civil market. It was however purchased by the Italian Air Force which uses it for multiple tasks. PD808GE MM61955 is operated by 14 *Stormo* from its base at Pratica di Mare. Its role is electronic warfare training.

Right: Pilatus PC6B Turbo Porter No. 889, of the French Army is seen at Fairford, July 1999. The length of the nose of the turboprop is apparent in this view.

Below: Developed from the earlier Nord 260 the **262 Fregate** is a twin-engine, high-wing light transport. It sold in both civil and military markets. No. 79 of 2S, French Navy, is seen departing Fairford, July 1985.

Above: Polish designed and built the PZL Wilga is an all-purpose light aircraft. Uses include parachute training, glider towing and liaison duties. **PZL 104A-35A Wilga** 75(Red) of DOSAAF is at Zhukovsky, August 1995.

Above: A general-purpose light transport of very rugged construction the Britten-Norman Islander has found many military customers. As well as a multi-role liaison aircraft it can be configured with underwing hard points for attack duties or with a nose radar for maritime patrol. **BN2A Islander** B-06 of the Belgian Army is at Middle Wallop, July 1982.

Above: A number of South American air forces operate airlines to go where the commercial airlines cannot afford to run services and do so in the public eye. The Iranian Air Force operates a cargo airline and keeps a very low profile. **Boeing 747-259F** EP-SHH/5-8114 of SAHA is seen at Sharjah, UAE, March 1997.

Below: The most important VIP operation in Britain used to be that of the Queen's Flight of the RAF. The four-engine safety of the type was a factor in the selection of the de Havilland Heron for the unit's operations. **Heron CC3** XH375 is at Odiham, September 1966, in a very bright colour scheme. (AG)

Above: The **Cessna 210 Centurion** is a 4/6-seat, high-wing (no strut) single-engined touring aircraft designed for the civil market. Some military use can be found. FAB 228 of the Bolivian Air Force is at La Paz, November 1992.

Left: Brazil's **Bandeirante** has been a great hit as a feedliner for civil transport. Its military uses are many, either as a 'standard' light transport or as a specialist multi-role with hardpoints and radars. FAC 1271 of the Colombian Air Force is on the ramp at Bogotá, September 1997. It is operated from there by Esc 712 as a transport.

Right: The de Havilland DH114 Heron is a big brother to the Dove. It is longer by ten feet and has four engines. They have been used for VIP roles and as illustrated by the RNAS Yeovilton station flight. **Sea Heron C1** XR442 was photographed at Lee-on-Solent in July 1987.

Below: The 125 is also used as a VIP aircraft for members of the royal household and government ministers. **BAe 125 CC3** ZD703 of 32 (The Royal) Squadron arrives at Fairford, July 1999. This unit, which has been flying VIPs for many years, adopted the new title when the Queen's Flight was abolished.

Below: On some occasions government ministers want to arrive with a low profile. This 32 Squadron aircraft has the colours toned down as well as unpublished self-defence systems. **BAe 125 CC3** ZE395 is at Fairford, July 1991.

Above: As with many air arms and business jets, the 125 has been used for a multitude of tasks. RAE Bedford used **DH(HS) 125 1B** XW930 for flight systems development, note the nose probe. It is seen arriving at Fairford, July 1985.

Below: The **SAAB T17 Supporter** is used by the Danish Air Force flying school at Karup to screen pilots for all three services. The type can and has been fitted with hard points for an offensive role. T427 is at Mildenhall, May 1992.

Below: Built at Prestwick by Scottish Aviation the **Twin Pioneer** was a rugged STOL light transport. With a fixed undercarriage it was powered by two Alvis Leonides 640 hp air-cooled radial piston engines. Operated by the RAF it mainly served east of Suez. The last British military operator was the Empire Test Pilots School. This gave pilots a chance to fly a type they would not be at all familiar with. XT610 is at Greenham Common, July 1973.

Below: In service since 1966, the de Havilland (now BAe) Dominie is a variant of one of the early business jets, the DH125. Its role within the RAF is that of a navigation trainer. The equipment fitted for this task has been updated over the years to reflect the types of aircraft that the trainees will fly in when qualified. **Dominie T1** XS712/A of 6 FTS is at Valley, August 1973 in the red/white training colours.

Left: The Beagle 206 was a British made 5/8-seat cabin monoplane powered by a pair of Rolls-Royce Continental piston engines. Twenty were built for the RAF as the **Basset CC1** and they were used by a number of communications squadrons. XS770 was the last on charge being used by the A&AEE at Boscombe Down. It is pictured at Finningley, September 1984.

Right: Noted for its swept-forward wings the **HFB 320 Hansa** is a business jet with a military role. This was one of ECM duties with the *Luftwaffe*. **Hansa ECM** 16+28 of Jbg 32 is at Mildenhall, May 1992.

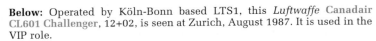

Below: Operated by Köln-Bonn based LTS1, this *Luftwaffe* Canadair CL601 Challenger, 12+02, is seen at Zurich, August 1987. It is used in the VIP role.

Above: Built by Morane-Saulnier, the MS760 Paris is a four-seat, twinjet liaison aircraft. The powerplants are a pair of 882 lb (400 kg) Turbomeca Marbore turbojets. No. 33/F-YETD is operated by the French Navy in a liaison role and is pictured at Greenham Common, July 1974.

Below: One of the most stylish aircraft in military liaison work is the Piaggio P180 Avanti. The wing is set at the rear fuselage with foreplanes on the nose; much use is made of carbon fibre in the construction. MM62164 of the Italian Air Force Test Centre (RSV) is at Yeovilton, July 1994.

Above: First flown as a twin, production Lockheed Jetstars have four rear-mounted engines. The type is used for among other tasks the transport of VIPs. C140B 61-2491 of the 58th MAS is at Greenham Common, July 1983.

Below: In full camouflage colours C140B Jetstar 59-5962 of 1866th Flight Checking Squadron of the Air Force Communications Service departs Fairford, July 1985. This unit, based at Scott AFB, IL, had five aircraft for calibration duties.

Above: The Danish Air Force operates examples of both the top of the range business jets. Pictured is VIP-configured Canadair CL604 Challenger C-066 of Esk 721, based at Vaerlose. It is seen at Fairford, July 1999.

Right: Turkish Air Force unit 224 Filo flies a number of different types of aircraft, both fixed and rotary wing. Seen at its Ankara–Etimesgut base is Cessna 560 Citation 93-7026. This design is one of the smaller range of business jets. It was photographed in May 1998. (PJD)

Below: Seen at Lemoore, CA (October 1979) is this US Navy **RU9D Aero Commander** from China Lake. It is an ex-USAF aircraft and carries the serial 576184 in a navy style.

Above: **Cessna's 550 Citation** is an earlier model of the 560 and has many differences. U20-03 01-407 of Spanish Navy unit Esc 004 is seen on a visit to Yeovilton from its base at Rota, July 1994.

Left: At one time practically every RAF base operated an aircraft as the 'Station Flight'. During the 1950s and 1960s it was most likely to be an Avro Anson. This type had served well as early variants joined RAF service in 1936. **Anson C19** VL306 of Waddington Station Flight is at Odiham, September 1964. (AG)

Below: **Avro Anson C19** VM352 can claim to have been the last Anson in British military service. It was operated by RAE Llanbedr (note the Welsh dragon on nose) and is pictured at Boscombe Down, March 1971.

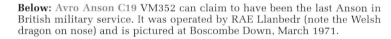

Above: The ETPS at Boscombe Down used a pair of Viscounts for both training test pilots and for transporting the class to visit other sites. **Viscount 744** XR801 is at its base, March 1971.

Left: Military use of the Vickers Viscount has been low. In the UK they have been used in small numbers as trials aircraft. **Viscount 837** XT575 is from RAE Bedford and used as a radar test bed. Note the dish under the front fuselage. It is pictured at Fairford, July 1985.

Right: This **Aero Commander 695**, FAC 5553, is used for VIP transport by the Colombian Air Force. It is at Bogotá, September 1997.

Right: Following the transport version, the next service variant of the Valetta was a flying classroom for navigation training. Valetta T3 WJ478/T is at Odiham, September 1966. Note the four astrodomes on the cabin roof. (AG)

Above: A military variant of the Vickers Viking airliner, the Valetta was used by the RAF in Transport Command. The main difference between the types was that the Valetta had a strengthened floor and a cargo-loading door. As with a number of types the A&AEE was the last user. Valetta C1 WJ491 is at its Boscombe Down base, March 1971.

Below: Boeing's 727 model made record sales in the civil market but few military ones. A mix of both is Ecuadorian Air Force airline TAME (*Transportes Aereos Mercantiles Ecuatorianos*). Its task is to run services that may not appeal to commercial operators, although this does not apply to all routes flown. Boeing 727-134 HC-BLF is at Latacunga AFB, September 1997.

Below: The Vickers Varsity was used as an advanced trainer for pilots converting to heavy multi-engined types and to train bomb aimers. To facilitate this latter task the under fuselage pannier had a bomb aiming position together with rear doors for practice bombs. WF331/M Varsity of 5 FTS is at Valley, August 1973.

Below: New Zealand's air force operates a pair of 727s in a mix of transport and VIP roles. Boeing 727-22C NZ7271 of 40 Squadron, based at Auckland, is seen at Boscombe Down, June 1992.

Above: The sole American military use of the 727 is with the Air National Guard Bureau. C22B 83-4616 is operated by 113th FW/201st AS at Andrews AFB, MD. It is pictured at Fairford, July 1989. Note the lack of titles on this aircraft.

Left: Sold to only two air arms (Jordan & Malaysia) the Handley Page Herald was marketed as a Dakota replacement. A high-wing, twin Rolls-Royce Dart powered airliner, it was the least successful, in sales terms, of that class of aircraft. HPR7 Herald 401 FM-1024 of the Royal Malaysian Air Force is seen at Farnborough prior to delivery, September 1964. (AG)

Below: Built in Israel, the IAI Arava is a light, twin-boomed, fixed-undercarriage cargo transporter with rough field capability. It has sold well in Central and South America. FAG 880 of the Guatemalan Air Force is at Prestwick, October 1976.

Below: With the same powerplant and a similar size and layout, except for the twin tail fins, the Max Holste MH1512M Broussard was the French equivalent of the Beaver. No. 18 is seen at Châteaudun, June 1977.

Above: IAI Arava 201 GN8595 is operated by the Venezuelan National Guard, part of the army. It is at Miranda AFB, Caracas, November 1992. This unit operates its aircraft in full colour markings.

Above: Sweden has produced a complete AWACs package. This Swedish Air Force SAAB 340 has been mated with sideways-looking Ericsson airborne reconnaissance radar. Tp100 Argus 100003 of F16M from Malmslatt is at Fairford, July 1998.

Left: The Reims Aviation-Cessna F406 Caravan II is a twelve-seat-plus utility transport powered by two P&W (Canada) PT6s. No. 0010 is operated by French Army unit 3eGHL. It is used to train anti-aircraft gunners by towing targets on the end of a cable up to seven kilometres long. It is pictured at Boscombe Down, June 1992.

Below: Seen here in an all-over camouflage is IAI Arava FAC 1952 of the Colombian Air Force. It is on the ramp at Bogotá, September 1997.

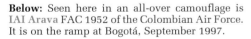

Right: This SAAB 340 (Tp100) of Swedish Air Force unit F16 is configured for passenger carriage. It is at Fairford, July 1995.

Right: Piston power in the US ANG units came to an end with a programme called ANGOSTA (ANG Operational Support Turboprop Aircraft). Beginning in 1987 C131s were replaced with Beech C12s or as illustrated a **Fairchild C26A Metro**. 86-0455 of the 103rd TASS Pennsylvania ANG is at London, Ont, June 1990. The unit was equipped with OA10As with the Metro acting as a unit liaison aircraft.

Below: The Czech-built LET 410 Turbolet was built in large numbers following its adoption by the Soviet airline Aeroflot as its standard feeder liner. Many Eastern Bloc air forces also used it in a variety of roles. When the two German states reunited the *Luftwaffe* took over a number of former GDR machines. 53+09 **LET 410UVP** of 3 LTS/FBS from Berlin/Tegal is at Fairford, July 1998.

Below: Powered by a single PT6A turboprop the **Socata TBM700** is a seven-seat passenger liaison aircraft. No. 99 is a French Army (*l'Armée de Terre*) example at Fairford, July 1997.

Above: First flown as long ago as 1945 the de Havilland DH104 Dove sold well to both civil and military operators. **Dove 8A** 201 of the Irish Air Corps is at its Baldonnel/Casement base, August 1977.

Below: In Swedish Air Force service each aircraft is given a specific type number. The Fairchild Metro is known as **Tp88**. 88003 of the FMV, at Malmslätt, is seen in its all-over camouflage at Ljungbyhed, August 1996. (PJD)

Below: Replacing HS748s the BAe 146 joined the then Queen's Flight of the RAF in 1986. The military fit includes infra-red jamming devices. **BAe 146 CC2** ZE701 is seen landing at Liverpool–Speke, March 1991 with HM Queen Elizabeth II onboard.

Below: Known as the Devon in RAF service the Dove was used as a utility passenger transport. Last in service was **Devon C2** VP981 of the Battle of Britain Memorial Flight. Its task was to act as a crew ferry and to take ground engineers to the locations that the historic aircraft were operating from. It is pictured at its Conningsby base, June 1989.

Left: A versatile type such as the LET 410 comes in different variants. Illustrated is a **LET 410FG** with a glass nose for survey work. 1523 is operated by 344 PZDLT of the Czech Air Force. It is at Hradec Králové, August 1998. (PJD)

Below: The **LET 610** is a bigger development of the 410; the same basic layout is kept but scaled up. 0005 of the Czech Air Force is at Zhukovsky, August 1995.

Below: Currently the best selling airliner in the world, in volume terms, is the Boeing 737. Military use is low. The USAF operates a navigator training aircraft based upon the 200 series. Inside are console stations for twelve trainees. **T43A** 73-1151 of the 323rd FTW, based at Mather AFB, CA, is at Travis AFB, CA, October 1979.

Below: The first of the jet powered Gulfstreams was the Gulfstream 2. Powered by a pair of Rolls-Royce Speys, it set new standards in business and VIP travel. The US Coast Guard operates a single model. Based at Washington National for VIP operations **VC11A** 01 is pictured at Paris, June 1977.

Above: Gulfstream stretched the G3 by 54 inches (1.37 m), changed the engines from the Rolls-Royce Spey to the Tay and called it the **Gulfstream 4**. The Irish Air Corps operates a single example in a VIP role; 251 is seen at Liverpool–Speke, April 1993.

Above: Seen here at Williams Gateway, AZ in October 1998 is **C20F (Gulf 4)** 91-0108 operated by the US Army for VIP work. The titles are 'United States of America', a style used by a number of VIP types.

Below: Using the same configuration as the Gulf 2 the **Gulfstream 3** featured a 23-inch (61 cm) stretch and an improved wing with winglets. The main military use is either VIP or multi-role missions. F-313 of Danish Air Force squadron Esk 721 is at Fairford, July 1995. As well as VIP use it can be found on SAR and fishery patrol flights.

Above: The BAC111 airliner has been used by the British military in test and trial roles. RAE Bedford operates **BAC111 Series 201** XX105. It is seen departing Fairford, July 1985.

Right: The Douglas Dakota has been and still remains one of the most important transport aircraft ever. Its roles have included every use an aeroplane can be put to. Still in service with the RAF is Dakota C3 ZA947. It is on charge to the BBMF as a support aircraft and as a training machine for potential Lancaster pilots. It is pictured in a wartime colour scheme at Fairford, July 1996.

Below: With a fleet of three aircraft, 4 Squadron of the Royal Air Force of Oman operates the BAC111 in a passenger transport role from its base at Seeb. BAC111-485GD 551 is at Fairford, July 1991.

Below: With the radar nose of an F104 Starfighter this Canadian Armed Forces Dakota was bound to be named 'Pinocchio'. CT129 12859 (the C47 was re-designated for CAF) is at Abbotsford, BC, August 1986.

Above: Seen here in a wonderful day-glo colour scheme is EC47 Dakota MM61893 14-46 of 14 *Stormo*, Italian Air Force. This aircraft was used for the calibration of navigation aids. It is pictured at Fairford, July 1985.

Below: Colombia operates a variety of Dakota variants. C47 FAC 1670 is in the cargo role at Madrid AFB, September 1997.

Above: Seen landing at Athens in June 1993 is Douglas C47 Dakota KN575 of the Greek Air Force. This air arm still operates the type for assorted duties. This particular aircraft was supplied to the Greeks by the RAF in May 1957 and has kept its original serial.

Below: Seen here at Lima in September 1997 is C47 Dakota AT521 of the Peruvian Navy. This service used the type for coastal patrol work as well as transport duties.

Left: A complete new lease of life came to the Dakota with the fitment of turboprops. Basler of Oshkosh WI is one of the leading companies converting airframes. This consists of a 40-inch (1.02 m) forward fuselage extension and the fitting of a pair of P&W PT6A engines. Basler Turbo 67 FAC 1681 is operated by the Colombian Air Force as a flying gunship. It is seen in its low visibility markings at Gomez AFB, Apiay, September 1997.

Below: As a civil aircraft the tall tailed Super Dakota was a flop; there were too many C47s on the market at low prices following World War II for people to buy a new type. The US Navy came to the rescue and ordered it in quantity. They operated it in a transport role for many years. C117D 17191 of NAS Mildenhall is seen at its base, May 1969.

Above: Following release from USN/USMC service C117s were mainly sold to small civil cargo/passenger carriers. A few found more work in military marks. FAC 1632 is operated by the Colombian Air Force at Madrid AFB, September 1997.

Above: The Royal Air Force operates a number of Lockheed L1011 TriStars in the tanker/transport role. TriStar K1 ZD949 of 216 Squadron is at Liverpool–Speke, February 1988.

Above: When the call to arms came for the 1991 Gulf War two of 216 Squadron's TriStars were painted desert pink for tanking operations. TriStar K1 ZD951 is at Fairford, July 1991.

Above: The Ilyushin IL-76 (NATO code-name Candid) was developed to replace or supplement the huge fleet of An-12s in service with the Soviet Air Force. IL-76MD UR76413 of the Ukrainian Air Force is at Fairford, July 1997.

Above: Ilyushin IL-76s have been exported to a small number of countries. K2661/A of the Indian Air Force is at Moscow Bykovo, August 1995. This air arm has twenty-four of the type in two squadrons and operates it under the name *Gajraj* (King Elephant).

Right: The airtanker variant of the IL-76 is the IL-78 (NATO code-name Midas). It is capable of refuelling three aircraft at once. 34(Blue) is a Russian Air Force example seen at Fairford, July 1993.

Right: When the Russians looked for a replacement for the Tupolev Tu-126 (Moss) AWACs platform the **IL-76** was selected as it had the space for all the required fittings of such a craft. The aircraft is a co-design with Beriev and has the designation **A-50** (NATO code-name Mainstay). 51(Red) is at Zhukovsky, in August 1995.

Below: An off-the-shelf type, the Douglas DC10 was selected to provide the USAF with a strategic tanker with added transport capability. Known as the KC10 Extender it first entered service in 1981. **KC10A** 82-0190 of the 2nd BW is at Mildenhall, May 1985.

Above: Two DC10s were acquired from Dutch carrier Martinair and converted to the tanker/transport role. Unlike the KC10 these Royal Dutch Air Force examples do not have a boom operator at the rear of the aircraft. The boom is controlled from the cockpit by remote video. **KDC10** T-264 of 334 Squadron is at Fairford, July 1996.

Left: Seen here in its bright-yellow colour scheme is **de Havilland (Canada) DHC 5 Buffalo** 115462 CC115 (CAF designation) at Hamilton, Ont, June 1990. The Buffalo is one of a long line of tough go-anywhere STOL transports built and operated in Canada.

Above: Camouflage soon covered the USAF fleet. **KC10A** 85-0029/SJ of the 4th Wing Seymour Johnson AFB, SC is pictured at Tyndall AFB, FL, April 1994.

Above: **CC115 Buffalo** 115460 of 424 Squadron, CAF is seen in a white scheme at Mildenhall, August 1980. The unit was based at Trenton.

Left: First in a line of Canadian STOL twins the **de Havilland DHC4 Caribou** took to the air in July 1958. Ordered in quantity by the US Army it was the largest type they flew. 60-3767 C7A of the California National Guard is at Madera, August 1986.

Below: Purchased in 1976 to replace its C47s the Togo Air Force obtained two **DHC 5 Buffalos**. 5V-MAG is seen at Paris–Orly, June 1977.

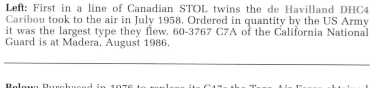

Below: Between 1965 and 1973 the Royal Thai Air Force purchased six new 748s. They are operated by 603 Squadron from Don Muang, Bangkok. **HS748-208** 99-999 is at its base, November 1999.

Below: In RAF service the 748 was known as the Andover. There were two distinct variants. **Andover CC2** XS793 of the Queen's Flight is at Finningley, September 1981. This model was a basic 748 with a VIP fit.

Left: The Andover C1 was a special military freighter. The entire rear end was redesigned to accommodate a rear-loading ramp that could open in flight to airdrop paratroopers or cargo. The undercarriage had a 'kneeling' facility to lower the loading ramp to floor level. **Andover C1** XS612 of 46 Squadron RAF is at Leuchars, September 1974.

Above: One of the successful 'Dakota Replacements' the Avro (Hawker Siddeley) 748 has sold well world-wide. Powered by a pair of Rolls-Royce Dart turboprops, it could operate from grass runways. **HS748-288** CS-03 of the Belgian Air Force is seen at Farnborough prior to delivery, September 1976. Note the cargo door is open in flight. The aircraft are used for either passenger or freight operations and are quickly converted to either role.

Left: **HS748-267** FAE 001/HC-AUK is part of the *Escuadron Presidencial* of the Ecuadorian Air Force. The configuration inside is quite basic with normal seats for the front 75% of the aircraft, with the remainder having eight wider seats in a blanked-off area at the rear. It is pictured at its Quito base, September 1997.

Right: Operated by 115 Squadron the **Andover E3A** was equipped as a navigation aid checker. XS644 is seen at Abingdon, September 1990.

Below: Operated by the US Army as a battlefield surveillance and intelligence gathering aircraft the **Grumman OV-1D** has been in service since 1961. As would be expected, systems have been updated over the years. 67-18898 of the 73rd Cbt 1Co departs Fairford, July 1985.

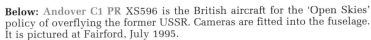

Below: The Transall C160 was a joint German/French transport aircraft powered by two Rolls-Royce Tyne turboprops. **C160D** 50+09 of *Luftwaffe* transport unit LTG 62 is at Brawdy, May 1980.

Below: **Andover C1 PR** XS596 is the British aircraft for the 'Open Skies' policy of overflying the former USSR. Cameras are fitted into the fuselage. It is pictured at Fairford, July 1995.

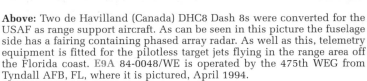

Above: Two de Havilland (Canada) DHC8 Dash 8s were converted for the USAF as range support aircraft. As can be seen in this picture the fuselage side has a fairing containing phased array radar. As well as this, telemetry equipment is fitted for the pilotless target jets flying in the range area off the Florida coast. **E9A** 84-0048/WE is operated by the 475th WEG from Tyndall AFB, FL, where it is pictured, April 1994.

Above: In the late 1970s France decided it needed more aircraft and re-opened the Transall production line. Twenty-five more aircraft were built as **C160NG**s (New Generation). Extra fuel tanks were added as was an in-flight-refuelling capability. F217 64-GQ of French Air Force transport unit ET64 is seen landing at Athens, June 1993.

Left: The **Sud-Ouest SO-30P Bretagne** was one of the first post-war French transport aircraft. It had a poor sales record in the civil market and most of the forty-five production aircraft were passed to the French military. No. 28 of the CEV is pictured at Odiham, September 1964. (AG)

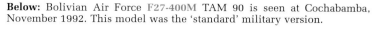

Below: Bolivian Air Force **F27-400M** TAM 90 is seen at Cochabamba, November 1992. This model was the 'standard' military version.

Above: The biggest French transport success, post-war, has been the **Sud Aviation SE210 Caravelle**. It sold mainly in the civil markets but was used for VIP operations by the French Air Force. No. 141 is at Odiham, September 1966. (AG)

Below: Designated **C31As** in US Army service two F27s are used by the 'Golden Knights' parachute display team. This unit is part of the 18th Aviation Brigade and based at Fort Bragg NC. 51608 is seen at Reno, NV, September 1988.

Above: During 1975 Fokker produced a Maritime Patrol F27. Equipped with search radar and a twelve-hour endurance it sold in small numbers. **F27-400MPA** D.2.01 802/10 is operated by Esc 802 of the Spanish Air Force. From its base at Gando in the Canary Islands it can cover a large area of the Atlantic Ocean. It is seen at Fairford, July 1996.

Above: Engine technology had evolved a great deal since the 1950s so in 1980 the USAF announced an upgrade in the KC135 powerplants. This involved fitting four CFM56 jets of 22,000 lb thrust; the original P&W J57 had 13,750 lb. **KC135R** 62-3554 of the 19th ARW departs Fairford, July 1989, showing the new, larger engines well.

Below: As a follow-on to the F27, Fokker produced the F50; the military version of this is the F60 Utility. This is a stretched airframe (64 inches/1.62 m) with new generation P&W Canada PW125 turboprops. **Fokker 60U** U.04 of 334 Squadron, Royal Dutch Air Force, is at Fairford, July 1996.

Above: The **Fokker F27 Friendship** has been the most successful of the western 'Dakota Replacements'. It is operated by the air arms of twenty-two nations. Some are special military variants others are civil aircraft in uniform. C-10 is an **F27M** Troopship of 334 Squadron, Royal Dutch Air Force. This version has a cargo floor and large freight door. It is at Greenham Common, July 1974.

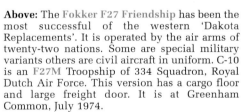

Above: Imperial Iranian Air Force **F27-400M** 5-218 is in desert camouflage. It is seen at Farnborough prior to delivery, September 1974.

Below: With such a high number of C135 airframes available many have been used for test and trial purposes. NKC135A 55-3129 of NASA Dryden has winglets fitted as well as a large nose probe. It is at Edwards AFB, October 1979. The 'N' in the designation indicates the conversion is of such a degree that it is not economical to return the aircraft to its original state.

Right: America's 'Open Skies' aircraft for the verification of the Arms Treaty is this OC135B. Packed with cameras it is operated by 24th RS/55th Wing. 61-2674 is at Mildenhall, May 1995.

Above: With a production run of 800+ airframes the Boeing C135 was a massive boost to the 707 programme. First flown in August 1956 the KC135A tanker was the most important variant with 732 built. KC135A 60-0320 of the 93rd BW is at its home base, Castle AFB, CA, October 1979.

Below: EC135N 60-0374 of ASD can be seen to have a huge nose extension. This contained a parabolic dish antenna and was used as a range instrumentation aircraft for the American space programme. It is photographed at Eglin AFB, FL, October 1981.

Above: EC135H 61-0282 of the 10th ACCS is pictured at Mildenhall, August 1976. The EC135 is a flying command post with an extensive communications suite for a senior officer to link with national command structure in times of crisis.

Above: To provide the special JP7 fuel for the Lockheed SR71 reconnaissance aircraft fifty-six KC135s were converted to KC135Q standard. This modification required the tanker's own fuel supply of JP4 to be isolated from the fuel the tanker could dispense. KC135Q 58-0089 of the 17th BW is at Mildenhall, August 1976.

Below: The RC135 range of aircraft are specialised reconnaissance variants. They are involved in such things as signals gathering, which can include radar and missile frequencies. Each aircraft seems to have a particular modification for its role. RC135V 64-14844/OF is operated by 55th Wing from Offutt AFB, NB. It is pictured at Mildenhall, May 1995. Note the extended nose and slabside fuselage fairing.

Below: Old civil Boeing 707s have been bought in and converted to E8C J-Stars (Joint Surveillance Target Attack Radar System) aircraft. The purpose of this mission is to detect ground traffic movements of enemy armour and convoys. It has a range of over 100 miles (161 km). The radar is housed in a long 'canoe'-like fairing under the fuselage. 92-3289/WR of the 93rd ACW is at Farnborough, September 1996.

Left: The **E6A Mercury** is the US Navy replacement for the EC130Q in the TACAMO (Take-Charge and Move Out) role of communicating with ballistic missile submarines. It carries an aerial which when deployed is 26,000 feet (7925 m) long for very low frequency transmissions. 164410 E6A of VQ4 is at Fairford, July 1998.

Below: Boeing 707s are used by many air forces world-wide for transport duties. Some were bought new, others as ex-civil airliners. **Boeing 707-3J9C** 5-249 in the former category, is an Imperial Iranian Air Force example. It is seen at Farnborough, September 1976.

Above: Seen here in low-visibility markings is Italian Air Force **Boeing 707-382B** MM62148 14-01 of 14 *Stormo*. Based at Pratica di Mare it is a tanker/transport. In its civil life it was an Air Portugal airliner. It was photographed at Fairford, July 1995.

Above: South African Air Force **Boeing 707-344** AF-617 is an ex-Air France aircraft. Now operated by 60 Squadron at Waterkloof it is an air tanker with a three-point hose and drogue system. It is pictured at Fairford, July 1995.

Left: It is logical that an ex-Qantas aircraft should be operated by the Royal Australian Air Force. **Boeing 707-338C** A20-623 is operated by Richmond-based 33 Squadron in the tanker/ transport role. Note the wing-mounted hose and drogue unit. It is seen at Boscombe Down, June 1992.

Below: *Luftwaffe* **Boeing 707-307C** 10+02 was bought new in 1968. Used in the transport role, it is seen at Winnipeg, June 1990.

Below: World Airways was the first user of this particular **Boeing 707-373C**. Now FAC 1201 of the Colombian Air Force it is at Bogotá, November 1992.

Right: Used as a crew trainer for its AWACS fleet, NATO Boeing 707-329C LX-N19996 was first used by Belgian airline SABENA. It is at Fairford, July 1995.

Above: American Airlines was the original owner of this *Grupo* 8 Boeing 707-323C of the Peruvian Air Force. FAP 319/OB-1371 is at its Lima base, September 1997.

Above: Western Airlines supplied this Boeing 707-347C to the Canadian Armed Forces. CC-137 13703 of 437 Squadron is a tanker/transport. It is pictured at Fairford, July 1995.

Above: Operated by 12 Squadron at Chakala this is Pakistan Air Force Boeing 707-340C 68-19866. It is an ex-Pakistan Airlines machine and is pictured landing at Manchester–Ringway, April 1989.

Below: The French were a buyer of the pure KC135 tanker. Most have been re-engined with CFM56s. C135FR No. 472 93-CC of ERV 93 is at Fairford, July 1995.

Below: The most distinctive Boeing 707 variant is the AWACS (Airborne Warning and Control System). The rotodome above the fuselage 30 ft (9.14 m) in diameter houses the radar set. E3B 77-0356/OK of the 522nd ACW is at Tyndall, FL, April 1994. American AWACS airframes do not have the big fan engines.

Above: KE3A 1815 is operated by the Royal Saudi Air Force as a tanker to support its AWACS fleet and other combat aircraft. On charge to 18 Squadron at Riyadh it is seen at Mildenhall, May 1993.

Below: Brazilian airline Varig operated this Boeing 707-345C before it was transferred to the air force. FAB 2402 KC137 of 2/2 Group Transport is based at Galeao in a tanker/transport role. It is seen at Fairford, July 1995.

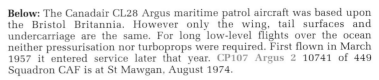

Below: The Canadair CL28 Argus maritime patrol aircraft was based upon the Bristol Britannia. However only the wing, tail surfaces and undercarriage are the same. For long low-level flights over the ocean neither pressurisation nor turboprops were required. First flown in March 1957 it entered service later that year. **CP107 Argus 2** 10741 of 449 Squadron CAF is at St Mawgan, August 1974.

Above: NATO operates a fleet of **E3A**s as a joint force venture. LX-N90442 is at Finningley, September 1984.

Below: Saudi Arabian **E3A** 1802 of 18 Squadron is seen at Boscombe Down, June 1992. This unit also operates the KE3A tankers.

Above: Known as the **Sentry AEW 1** in RAF service the fleet is jointly used by both 8 and 23 Squadrons. Based at Waddington ZH102 is seen at Cottesmore, June 1997.

Above: The Avro Shackleton was for many years the mainstay of Coastal Command patrolling the sea-lanes around Britain. It used the same wing as the Lincoln but had a new fuselage and Rolls-Royce Griffon engines with contra-rotating propellers. **Shackleton MR2** WR966 of O/204 Squadron is at Odiham, September 1964. (AG)

Below: **Shackleton MR3**s were a new variant featuring a tricycle undercarriage, extra range with tip tanks plus many other improvements. WR972, in the special colours of the Royal Aircraft Establishment, is at Boscombe Down, March 1971.

Above: Training for Shackleton crews was provided by the MOTU (Maritime Operational Training Unit) on the **T4** model. This variant had the armament removed and additional radar positions for trainees. WB820 of S/MOTU is at Odiham, September 1964. (AG)

Below: Seen here in standard markings of a white top over sea grey is **Shackleton MR3** XF708 of A/120 Squadron. Note the unit number is carried in large letters. It was photographed at Lakenheath, May 1965. (AG)

Right: Shackletons found a new lease of life when twelve were fitted with airborne early warning radar. The new variant was the **AEW 2** and has a large radome under the nose. They flew from 1972 with 8 Squadron. WL795 is pictured at Liverpool–Speke, June 1981.

Below: Lockheed's P3 Orion maritime patrol aircraft was developed from the L188 Electra airliner. It has matured into the most widely used ocean patroller in the world. **P3A** 152166 3/PG of VP65 is at Edwards AFB, October 1979. This US Navy reserve squadron, named 'The Tridents', is based at Point Magu, CA.

Below: As Orion production ran on, a new variant the P3B was introduced. Among many updates was the facility to fire the Bullpup air-to-surface missile. **P3B Orion** 153426 of reserve squadron VP93 'The Executioners' is at its base, Selfridge ANGB, MI, June 1990. Note that the colourful markings are beginning to disappear.

Above: A special Orion variant is the **EP3E**. This is an electronic reconnaissance/warfare aircraft whose role is to be able to determine the emissions of naval vessels. Note the under-fuselage radome. 150505 24/VQ2 is at Boscombe Down, June 1992. VQ2 'Batman' is based at NAS Rota, Spain.

Below: US Navy squadron VXN8, based at Patuxent River MD, is dedicated to airborne geophysical surveying, acting as an Oceanographic Development Unit. They fly a number of Orions in different modification states. 150528 05/JB is a **UP3A**. This variant is a P3A with ASW equipment removed and used as a utility transport. It sports the unit's distinctive colour scheme at its base, May 1989.

Above: The P3C became the definitive version of the Orion. This is still being updated with new equipment on a regular basis. **P3C** 158921 LF of VP16 'Eagles' is at Lakenheath, August 1975. This unit is based at Jacksonville, FL.

Below: Known in Canadian service as the **CP140 Aurora** the aircraft fleet is based at either side of that vast country in British Columbia or Nova Scotia. 140115 of 407 Squadron is seen on the ramp at its base at Comox, BC, May 2000.

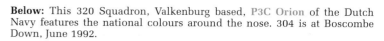

Below: This 320 Squadron, Valkenburg based, **P3C Orion** of the Dutch Navy features the national colours around the nose. 304 is at Boscombe Down, June 1992.

Above: This **P3B Orion** of 5 Squadron, Royal New Zealand Air Force is based at Auckland in North Island. NZ4203 is at Fairford, July 1989 in full colour markings including the Albatross insignia on the tail.

Below: The colours have been toned down in this Australian **P3C Orion**. It keeps the white top but national markings are in grey. A9-658 of Edinburgh SA based 11 Squadron is at Fairford, July 1989.

Above: Seen here in a two-tone grey with white undersides is Portuguese Air Force **P3P Orion** 14804 of Esq 601. It is pictured at its Montijo base, March 1997. (PJD)

Below: The **S3B Viking** is a reworked S3A with updated electronics. 160163 700/NE of VS38 'Red Griffins' is seen departing Elmendorf AFB, AK, May 2000. This unit is part of carrier air wing CVW 2 from USS *Constellation* (CV 64). It is of note in having the squadron badge in full colour on the tail. This marking is usually an indication of either the squadron CO or the ship's CAG aircraft.

Above: **Lockheed's S3 Viking** was designed as a carrier-based anti-submarine warfare aircraft. It was a replacement for the piston-engined Grumman Tracker. **S3A** 159751 700/AB of VS32 'Maulers' is at Mildenhall, August 1978.

Left: First flown in 1961 the **Breguet BR1150 Atlantic** has served five nations as a long range maritime patrol aircraft. No. 49 of French Navy squadron 21F, based at Nîmes/Garon, is at Mildenhall, May 1992.

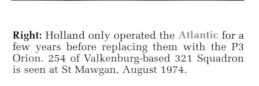

Right: Holland only operated the **Atlantic** for a few years before replacing them with the P3 Orion. 254 of Valkenburg-based 321 Squadron is seen at St Mawgan, August 1974.

Below: Conceived as a Shackleton replacement for the RAF the Nimrod was developed from the Comet airliner. Power was provided by four Rolls-Royce Spey engines making the Nimrod the only pure-jet maritime patrol aircraft. **Nimrod MR1** XV240 is at Valley, August 1975. This aircraft was based at Kinloss and as normal did not carry individual squadron markings, the aircraft being serviced centrally.

Above: An upgrade plan started in 1975 to bring the Nimrod MR1 up to a completely new avionics and systems fit. The addition of in-flight refuelling systems following the 1982 Falklands War brought the converted airframes to **Nimrod MR2P** standard. XV252 is at Cottesmore, June 1996 and shows the markings of Kinloss based 201 Squadron. This is an unusual addition to a Nimrod.

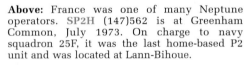

Below: The German Navy has been flying **Atlantics** since 1966. All the fleet is operated by MFG3 at Nordholz. 61+07 is seen flying at Greenham Common, July 1973.

Below: In Italy the air force supplies the flight crews and the navy the systems operators. **BR1150 Atlantic** MM40122 30-07 of 30 *Stormo* is at Boscombe Down, June 1992. This unit is based at Cagliari, Sardinia.

Above: France was one of many Neptune operators. **SP2H** (147)562 is at Greenham Common, July 1973. On charge to navy squadron 25F, it was the last home-based P2 unit and was located at Lann-Bihoue.

Below: From the late 1940s into the 1970s the **Lockheed P2 Neptune** served the US Navy as a maritime patrol aircraft in front-line and reserve squadron status. **P2H** 145905 (ex-P2V7) 7W is operated in the latter mode at Willow Grove NAS, PA, where it is pictured, August 1970. (SGW)

Below: Seen at a wet St Mawgan, August 1974 is Dutch Air Force **SP2H Neptune** 202 from 320 Squadron at Valkenburg. This was the last main production variant and had power boosted by two 3400 lb thrust Westinghouse J34 turbojets under the wings.

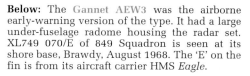

Below: The Gannet AEW3 was the airborne early-warning version of the type. It had a large under-fuselage radome housing the radar set. XL749 070/E of 849 Squadron is seen at its shore base, Brawdy, August 1968. The 'E' on the fin is from its aircraft carrier HMS *Eagle*.

Below: The Ilyushin IL-38 (NATO code-name May) is a development of the IL-18 airliner. It is a long-range maritime patrol aircraft with an endurance of twelve hours. 22(Red) of the Russian Navy Training Regiment at Ostrov is pictured at Fairford, July 1996.

Above: Grumman's HU16 Albatross was the largest and last in a line of amphibians. It first flew in 1947 and sold to many air arms. HU16B AD.1B-10 of Esc 801, Spanish Air Force, is at its Palma Majorca base, November 1973. The role of the unit was search and rescue.

Below: First flown in 1949 the Fairey Gannet was a carrier-borne anti-submarine aircraft powered by a single Armstrong Siddeley Double Mamba turboprop. Training variants were the T2 and T5. Gannet T5 XG883 733/BY of 849 Squadron is seen at its base, RNAS Brawdy, August 1968.

Below: The US Coast Guard operated more than eighty Albatross aircraft in an SAR role. HU16E 1293 is at Corpus Christie, TX, October 1976. (SGW)

Below: Norway used HU16s in a maritime patrol role until they were replaced in 1969 by P3 Orions. 17202 WH/B of 330 Skv, Bodø, is seen at St Mawgan, September 1964. (AG)

Below: One of the oldest designs currently flying off aircraft carriers is the Breguet BR1050 Alize. Operated by the French and Indian Navy, it is an ASW aircraft powered by a single Rolls-Royce Dart turboprop. No. 60 of 4F, French Navy, is seen at Mildenhall, May 1992.

Above: Each aircraft carrier had a dedicated aircraft for *ad hoc* parts and staff transport. These were known as COD – Carrier Onboard Delivery – flights. Gannet COD4 XG786 074/E from HMS *Eagle* is at its shore base, Brawdy, August 1968.

Right: The Grumman S2 Tracker was designed for a carrier-borne ASW track and attack role. It was exported to many nations. S2 Tracker 151 is a Valkenburg-based Dutch Navy example. These were flown off the carrier HRMS *Karel Doorman*. It is pictured at Brawdy, August 1968.

Above: Seen on the ramp at Jacksonville NAS, FL, July 1974 is US-2C Tracker 133359/JE of VC2 Det. JAX. This variant is a target-towing utility aircraft hence its bright colours. (SGW)

Above: Grumman produced a COD version of the Tracker; this was the C-1A Trader. It could carry either nine passengers or freight. 136753 of NAF Mildenhall is seen at Lakenheath, August 1975.

Below: Many earlier Trackers were stripped of the radar and weapons systems and had a second set of controls added for pilot training. TS-2A 136402/D of training squadron VT28 is at its Corpus Christie, TX base, October 1976. (SGW)

Above: Trackers were used by the Australian Navy when they had an aircraft carrier. The last one, HMAS *Melbourne*, was scrapped in 1983. S-2E N12-153598 841 of 816 Squadron is seen at Greenham Common, June 1977.

Below: The most radical development of the Tracker was the E-1B Tracer. This was a carrier-based airborne early warning aircraft. The radar, rotating at 6 rpm, was housed in a fixed 17 ft 6 in (5.33 m) diameter radome. E-1B 148912 701/GE of RVAW120 is at Norfolk NAS, VA, May 1972. (SGW)

Below: The current carrier-borne AWACS is the Grumman E2C Hawkeye. This is a turboprop powered by a pair of Allison T56s of 4910 shp. First delivered to the fleet in 1964 the basic shape has remained the same but the electronics have been improved beyond all recognition. E2C 159109 012/AD of VAW120 'Cyclones' is pictured at Hamilton, Ont, June 1990. This squadron is the East Coast Fleet Replenishment unit.

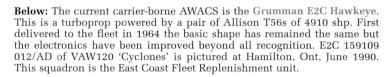

Right: The Westland Dragonfly was a British-built version of the Sikorsky S51. A single 550 hp Alvis Leonides piston engine provided power. Dragonfly HR5 WN500 904/BY is operated by RNAS Brawdy as a station flight aircraft; it is pictured there in July 1962. (AG)

Below: Westland in England built the H34 under licence as the Wessex. All the UK aircraft were powered by a Napier Gazelle gas turbine engine giving more power than piston H34s. Wessex HAS 3 XM927 660/PO from 737 Squadron, Royal Navy, is at Brawdy, May 1980. The HAS 3 was an anti-submarine strike helicopter armed with two homing torpedoes.

Below: One of the most successful helicopter designs was the Sikorsky H34 Choctaw. The users included the German Navy who operated it in the SAR role. SH34 80+94 of MFG5 is at Lee-on-Solent, July 1972.

Above: The Bristol Sycamore was the RAF's first British-designed helicopter. Duties included air-sea rescue from locations around the British Isles. Sycamore HR14 XJ917 S-H of the CFS is at its Ternhill base, September 1963. (AG)

Above: With the Hawkeye in service a COD version was soon developed. This was much needed as the previous COD aircraft, the Trader, had piston engines and thus ran on petrol. No current carrier-based aircraft used this type of fuel and so ships stopped tanking it. The Trader was range-limited as it had to depart its shore base and fly to and from the carrier without being able to fill its tanks. The Greyhound, as the new aeroplane was called, was a much bigger airframe and could carry up to thirty-nine passengers. C2A Greyhound 162140 of the Naval Air Test Centre is seen at its Patuxent River, MD base, May 1989.

Above: Sud Aviation in France licence built the H34. Belgium was one of the recipients of these. H34A B5/OT-ZKE of 40 *Heli-Smaldeel* is at Lee-on-Solent, July 1972.

Right: RAF use of the Wessex was two-fold. First there was the troop/cargo carrier for the Army and the other role was the SAR. Wessex HC2 XS679 WG/2 FTS is at Waddington, July 1993. Shawbury-based 2 FTS was the RAF's rotary-wing training unit.

Below: Operated by Portland NAS as an SAR helicopter, **Wessex HAS1** XS888 420/PO of 737 Squadron is seen at Lee-on-Solent, July 1972.

Above: Yellow helicopters were one of the RAF's best known sights as they were seen rescuing people in distress around the country. **Wessex HC2** XR588 of 22 Squadron is at Finningley, September 1990. With an SAR role, this unit had flights based at locations around the UK.

Above: Developed as an assault helicopter for the Royal Marines the **Wessex HU5** could go into action with guns or wire-guided air-to-surface missiles. Wessex HU5 XS479 V/V of 848 Squadron, Royal Navy, is at Valley, August 1975. This unit was based on HMS *Bulwark*.

Above: Twenty-six Lynx helicopters were purchased by the French Navy. Roles include anti-submarine operations with a dunking sonar. **Lynx HAS 2(FN)** No. 622 of 34F is at Middle Wallop, July 1984.

Above: Holder of the helicopter world speed record, the Westland Lynx is currently one of the best selling multi-role rotary-wing craft on the market. There are two main versions, the land and the shipboard. **Lynx AH1** XZ182 23A of 3 CBAS Royal Marines is at Mildenhall, May 1986. Land variants up to the Mark 9 had skid undercarriages.

Above: This Navy Lynx is defined by a wheeled undercarriage. The type is used to operate off small ships and can carry a range of guns and missiles together with more and more improved avionics. **Lynx HAS 3** ZD262 632/PO is operated by the then Portland-based 702 Training Squadron. It is pictured at Abingdon, September 1990.

Below: Denmark uses its Navy Lynxes in a fishery protection role — they are not armed. **Lynx Mk 80** S-134 of Esc 722 is at Mildenhall, May 1992.

Above: Seen at Fassberg, June 1983 is a German Navy **Lynx HAS 88**, 83+12 of MFG3. They operate aboard frigates with the prime task of anti-submarine warfare. Other roles such as SAR will be performed as required.

Below: Code-named Hind by NATO the Mil Mi-24 is a heavy attack helicopter with troop-carrying capability. It has nose-mounted guns and stub wing with hard points for a vast selection of rockets, bombs, etc. **Mi-24D** 0703 of 331 VRLT, Czech Air Force, is at Fairford, July 1995.

Above: The Saro Skeeter was a two-seat light helicopter used mainly by the Army Air Corps. Three served with the RAF. Skeeter T13 XM556/V of the CFS Rotary Wing is at its base, Ternhill, September 1963. (AG)

Below: Developed from the Russian Mi-2 the Polish PZL W-3 Sokol is a new design. Although larger, it has the same basic outline. PZL W3W 0810 of 2 PHSZ, Polish Army, is at Kraków/Balice, April 1998. (PJD)

Below: One of the largest European helicopters, the Aérospatiale SA3210 Super Frelon is used by the French Navy for ship-borne logistical support. No. 148 of 32F is at Middle Wallop, July 1982.

Below: With the Mi-8 being built in vast numbers there are lots of upgrades and sub types. 08(Yellow) of the Russian Air Force is at Tushino, August 1995. This is a Hip-C with five rotor blades.

Above: Russia's Mil Mi-8 &17 (NATO code-name Hip) range of medium transport helicopters are to be found in the air arms of over fifty countries. **Mi-8S** 94+12 of MF1, German Navy, is at Boscombe Down, June 1992. These aircraft were acquired with the reunification of Germany but were soon disposed of.

Right: Mi-8T 628 of 36 SPLT is operated as a transport helicopter by the Polish Air Force. It is pictured at Kraków/Balice, April 1998. (PJD)

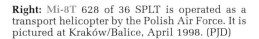

Right: Seen with its back doors open is **Mi-17** EJC 175 of the Colombian Army. This is the only helicopter operated by the army. It is at Bogotá, September 1997.

Above: This Peruvian Air Force **Mi-17** carries both civil and military identities. FAP 662/OB-1575 is operated by *Grupo* 3 from its base at Lima where it was pictured, September 1997.

Below: Used as a communications jammer, note the antenna array on the side, **Mi-17 PPA** 707 is operated by 87HE, Hungarian Air Force. It is pictured at Szentkiralyszabadja, September 1997. (PJD)

Above: Built under licence from Aérospatiale the **Westland Gazelle** serves in all the UK armed services. **Gazelle HT3** XW852 of 32 Squadron RAF is used as a VIP transport. It is pictured at Fairford, July 1987.

Above: Seen on the ramp at Zokniai, May 1995 is **Mi-8** 01(Blue) of 13 Squadron, Lithuanian Air Force. (JDS)

Below: **Gazelle AH1** XZ347/T of 9 Regiment, Army Air Corps, is seen at Boscombe Down, June 1992. The sand colour relates to its use in the Gulf War.

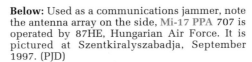

Left: Used by the Fleet Air Arm for pilot training, **Gazelle HT2** XW863 42/CU of 705 Squadron is at Mildenhall, June 1984.

Below: The Ecuadorian Army operates French-built **SA342 Gazelle** E373. It is pictured at Quito, September 1997.

Above: The replacement for the Sea King in Royal Navy service is to be the **Westland Merlin HM1**. ZH826 is operated by 700M Squadron, the Fleet Air Arm trials unit for the type. It is pictured at Fairford, July 1999.

Left: Bell's **204/UH1 Iroquois** was the most widely produced western helicopter. For many people the sight of one flying with its heavy blade sound is the image of the war in Vietnam. Seen in the last days of full colour US Army markings is 43697 of the 'Flying Mustangs' at Heidelburg, July 1970. A matt-green over-all with black insignia colour scheme soon followed.

Above: Bolivia is another country to receive UH1s to stem the drugs tide. **UH-1H** FAB 722 is at Santa Cruz, November 1992. *Grupo Aereo* 51 operates them. The tail has the Bolivian colours on it.

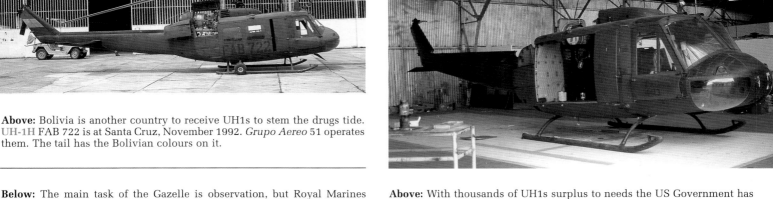

Below: The main task of the Gazelle is observation, but Royal Marines operations have included machine-guns and air-to-ground unguided rockets fired from out-rigger pods. **Gazelle AH1** XX412/Y 3 CBAS RM is at Yeovilton, August 1984.

Above: With thousands of UH1s surplus to needs the US Government has supplied them to friendly nations. Colombia is a recipient of these to help control the drug trade. **UH-1H** FAC 4413 is under maintenance at Madrid AFB, September 1997.

Above: Seen at Marana, AZ, October 1976, prior to delivery is **UH-1B** FAP-116 of the Panamanian Air Force. An ex-US Army helicopter, formerly 62-1895, it has a full colour scheme. (SGW)

Right: Dornier in Germany built over 300 UH1s for the *Luftwaffe* and German Army (*Heer*). **UH-1D** 72+59 of Army unit HFR 10 is at Fassberg, June 1983.

Left: Agusta in Italy licence built the UH1; these were known as the Agusta Bell AB204. Austria was the first country after Italy to acquire the type. **AB204B** 4D-BW of the 3rd Helicopter Squadron is at Hurn, July 1969. (SGW)

Above: Italian Air Force **AB204B** MM80331 15-26 of 15 *Stormo* is used in the SAR role. It is seen at Lee-on-Solent, July 1972.

Above: Both the Swedish Air Force and Army operated the **AB204B**s. They were given the local designation Hkp.3c. 03313 53/ of *Armeflyskolan* is at Middle Wallop, July 1984.

Above: The Bell 212 first flew in 1965, looking very similar to the 204. It was in fact twin-engined. Designated **UH-1N**, it was operated by all four of America's fighting services. US Navy UH-1N 160827 is based onboard USS *Guadalcanal* where it is pictured, October 1978.

Above: Used by the Italian Navy for anti-submarine warfare, the Agusta Bell AB212ASW featured a dome-shaped bulge on the cabin roof. As well as detecting submarines it could carry torpedoes or missiles for attack. MM80943 7-11 of *Gruppo* 4 is at Paris, June 1977. The AB212 is the Italian-built Bell 212.

Below: **AB402B**s were used by the Dutch Navy from 1961 to 1978 when they were replaced by the Westland Lynx. 228 from 7 Squadron, Valkenburg, is at Lee-on-Solent, July 1972.

Above: Operated by Colombian Air Force unit Esc 311 at Gomez Nino AFB, Bell 212 FAC 4005 has the name 'Juanito' on its nose. It is pictured at its base, September 1997.

Below: The **Bell 412** is a 212 with four rotor blades. This reduced vibration and noise. FAC 0004 of the Colombian Air Force Presidential Flight is at Bogotá, September 1997.

Above: Slovenia was once part of Yugoslavia but is now an independent state with a small air arm. **Bell 412EP** H2.35 of 15 *Brigada* is at Fairford, July 1999. The SFOR is the UN 'Stabilisation Force'.

Below: Bell stretched the 212 design by 8 ft (2.44 m) and installed two 2250 shp GE T700 turboshaft engines to produce the **Bell 214ST** (Super Transport). FAP 639/OB-1580 is operated by *Grupo* 3 of the Peruvian Air Force. It is at its Lima base, September 1997.

Below: 3 Squadron equipped with **AB412SPs** operates SAR duties for the Dutch Air Force at Leeuwarden. R.01 is pictured at Yeovilton, July 1994.

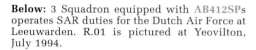

Below: **Sikorsky CH3E** 65-5697/LH is operated by 302nd SOS AFres at Luke AFB, AZ, October 1979. The H3 was a USAF variant of the SH3 with major design changes including a rear loading door and new undercarriage.

Above: The 412 is known in British service as the Griffin HT1. It is used for advanced helicopter training for Royal Air Force pilots only at RAF Shawbury. **Griffin HT1** ZJ237/T is operated by the Defence Helicopter Flying School. It is at Fairford, July 1997.

Right: Following replacement in the USAF with the CH53 the **Sikorsky HH3** long-range search and rescue helicopter was issued to two ANG units. **HH3E** 65-12781 of the 129th AR&RS California ANG is at Heywood, October 1979.

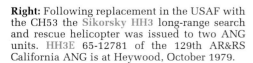

Below: Austria purchased two **CH53Cs** in 1970 and operated them for eleven years before selling them on to Israel. 5L-MA is at North Weald, May 1972.

Above: The German Army is a major **CH53** user with most of its aircraft assembled locally. 85+08 of HFTR 15 shows its lift capability with this underslung UH-1D at Fassberg, June 1983.

Above: Westland developed two helicopters side by side; they were the Scout for the Army and the Wasp for the Navy. Both were basically the same and were identified as 'A Wasp has wheels and a Scout has skids'. The Army Air Corps used the Scout as a general-purpose helicopter with the capability for firing anti-tank rockets. **Scout AH1** XP849 was passed on to the ETPS for test pilot training. It is pictured at Yeovilton, July 1994.

Below: Originally developed for the US Marine Corps as a heavy-lift helicopter the Sikorsky S65 attracted the attention of the USAF for a long-range rescue craft. **CH53C** 70-1631 of 1550th ATTW is at Biggs AAF, TX, October 1984. This Kirtland-based unit was tasked with rescue training.

Above: The Bell AH-1G Huey Cobra was developed for the US Army. The Marines wanted their own version; this was the AH-1J. The biggest change was that it was twin-engined, being powered by a pair of P&W (Canada) T400 turboshafts. **AH-1J** 159211 is at Miramar NAS, CA, October 1976. (SGW)

Above: Operated by 705 Squadron Fleet Air Arm for basic helicopter training, the **Hiller HT2** served in this role from 1963 until 1975. A single 305 hp Lycoming piston engine powered it. XS162 is at Portland, August 1974.

Below: Royal Navy use of the Wasp was as a light anti-submarine attack platform armed with homing torpedoes or depth charges. With a folding tail it flew from the rear decks of frigates. **Wasp HAS1** XS452 441 of 829 Squadron is based on HMS *Falmouth*. It is seen at Valley, August 1973.

Above: The **Boeing Vertol H46 Sea Knight** was produced for the US Marine Corps as an assault troop carrier. It could carry seventeen fully equipped Marines or a 4000 lb cargo load. CH46F 155313 1/YS of HMM162 is aboard USS *Guadalcanal*, October 1978.

Below: The H46 is operated by the Canadian Armed Forces as the **CH113A Labrador**. Its tasks are search and rescue. 11307 of 442 Squadron is seen at its home base Comox, BC, May 2000.

Below: Known in Swedish service as the Hkp4, this helicopter is a Japanese-built Boeing Vertol 107. The Swedish Navy operates **Kawasaki/ Vertol 107** 04063. Roles include anti-submarine operations and SAR. It is pictured at Middle Wallop, July 1984.

Above: With its big bubble cockpit the Bell 47G is one of the best-known helicopters in the world. It set many records and proved what a reliable machine it was. **OH-13H** 56-2166 of the US Army is at Heidelburg, July 1970. Army uses included observation and casualty evacuation.

Below: Licence-built by Westland the Bell 47 was known in the British military as the Sioux. Most went to the Army but a number of dual-control machines were operated by the RAF Central Flying School. **Sioux HT2** XV313 E/CFS is at Valley, August 1973.

Below: Since it first flew in 1961 the **Boeing Vertol H47 Chinook** has developed out of all recognition. Originally powered by two 2200 shp Lycoming T55 turboshafts the latest model has engines rated at 4500 shp, over twice the power. Avionics have also been upgraded. **CH47C** 4.201 of the Imperial Iranian Air Force is at Paris, June 1971. Most of the Iranian Chinooks went to the Army. (JDS)

Below: Operated by 1 *Reggimento* of the Italian Army at Viterbo **CH47C Chinook** MM80844 EI-822 is at Middle Wallop, July 1982. The type's roles include heavy transport and paratroop training.

Left: Operated by the RAF in support of the Army, British Chinooks have all been upgraded to the latest standards. **Chinook HC1** ZA707 EV/7 Squadron is flying at Finningley, September 1986.

Right: The largest user of the Chinook is the US Army. Seen flying over its home base of Fort Wainwright, AK, is **CH47D** 89-0171. This aircraft is operated by Co.B 4-123rd AVN. It is of note that the undercarriage has skis fitted to it to suit the severe climate of Alaska. It was photographed in May 2000.

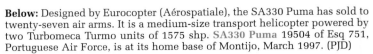

Below: Designed by Eurocopter (Aérospatiale), the SA330 Puma has sold to twenty-seven air arms. It is a medium-size transport helicopter powered by two Turbomeca Turmo units of 1575 shp. **SA330 Puma** 19504 of Esq 751, Portuguese Air Force, is at its home base of Montijo, March 1997. (PJD)

Above: Westland at Yeovil built the RAF Pumas. They are operated in support of the Army. **Puma HC1** XW220 of CZ/33 Squadron, in Gulf War desert colours, is at Fairford, July 1991.

Below: Known as the Hkp10 in Swedish service, the **Super Puma** is used for long-range SAR missions. 10412 89/F15 of the Swedish Air Force has bright colours for its rescue role. It is pictured at Fairford, July 1996.

Above: French Army **Puma** No. 1214/ADL of 6 ème RHC is seen at Fairford, July 1985. The French Army operates over 130 Pumas, obtaining the first in 1968. Over the years there have been many upgrades.

Below: Super Puma was the name given to the SA332. As its name implies it was a development with more powerful engines as well as many other modifications. **SA332M Super Puma** T-311 is operated by the Swiss Air Force in a transport role. It is pictured at Dübendorf, August 1987.

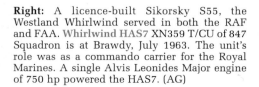

Above: RAF Whirlwind use was widespread and included a number with the Central Flying School for the training of flying instructors. **Whirlwind HAR10** XP360 WV/CFS is at Abingdon, June 1968.

Right: A licence-built Sikorsky S55, the Westland Whirlwind served in both the RAF and FAA. **Whirlwind HAS7** XN359 T/CU of 847 Squadron is at Brawdy, July 1963. The unit's role was as a commando carrier for the Royal Marines. A single Alvis Leonides Major engine of 750 hp powered the HAS7. (AG)

Below: Ordered by the USAF as a crash rescue and airborne fire fighter the Kaman H43 Huskie first flew in 1958. Powered by a single Lycoming T53 turboshaft of 860 shp the design had two intermeshing rotors. **HH43F** 59-1564 is at Lee-on-Solent, July 1972.

Above: Later versions of the Whirlwind were turbine-powered with a single Bristol Siddeley Gnome of 1050 shp. **Whirlwind HAR10** XP403 of 202 Squadron is in the famous yellow rescue colour. The winch can be seen over the doorframe. It is pictured at Finningley, July 1977.

Left: First flown in 1959 the Kaman H2 Seasprite serves to this day. The type's role on US Navy warships is anti-submarine. **VH2A Seasprite** 149032 HT/157 of HC4 is aboard USS *Guadalcanal*, August 1970.

Below: Seen at Middle Wallop, July 1982, is Agusta A109 AE-331/CC. The former operator was the Argentine Army who had it armed with rocket pods and miniguns. It had been captured at Port Stanley during the Falklands War the previous month. Later given the British serial ZE411 it operates today in a support role for the Special Forces.

Above: Built by Sud (now Aérospatiale), the Alouette II was a very successful general-purpose light helicopter. Purchased by over twenty-five countries military use includes casualty evacuation and observation. **SE3130 Alouette II** V-43 of the Swiss Air Force is at Dübendorf, August 1987.

Left: The Mil Mi-2 (NATO code-name Hoplite) helicopters were all manufactured by PZL in Poland. A light eight-passenger machine, it is the standard Russian training craft. 23(White) of the Russian support unit DOSAAF is at Monino, August 1991.

Right: The McDonnell Douglas (Hughes) AH64 Apache is one of the most advanced and formidable attack helicopters being built today. Its main weapon is up to sixteen Hellfire long-range laser-guided missiles for anti-tank duties. 22248, the YAH64A prototype, is seen at Middle Wallop, July 1982.

Below: Belgium's Navy operates just three Alouette IIIs for liaison work with ships and in an SAR role at Koksijide. M1/OT-ZPA is at Mildenhall, May 1996.

Below: Swiss Air Force Alouette IIIs are used for utility transport and SAR duties. A total of eighty-four were obtained in the early 1960s. SE3160 Alouette III V-260 is at Dübendorf, August 1987.

Above: Between 1963 and 1974 the Irish Air Corps obtained a total of eight Alouette IIIs. Roles included Army liaison and support as well as SAR duties. SE3160 Alouette III 196 is at Baldonnel/Casement, August 1977.

Below: Built on the success of the Alouette II came the Alouette III. It had a larger cabin, more powerful engine and improved equipment. The rear fuselage was covered-in. A-499 is a Dutch Air Force example operated by 'The Grasshoppers' display team. It is seen at Fassberg, June 1983.

Below: The German Army operated 300+ Alouette helicopters. Alouette II 76+85 of FTR10 is at Fassberg, June 1983.

Above: Seen at Lee-on-Solent, July 1972, is Alouette III M.019 of Esk 722, Danish Air Force. The type was later transferred to the Navy Flying Service. Note the large inflatable floats.

Left: Sikorsky won the competition to supply a UH1 replacement for the US Army. The new helicopter was the UH60 Blackhawk. Since entering service in 1979 the type has evolved and been exported. UH60L FAC 4122 of the Colombian Air Force is at Madrid AFB, September 1997.

Below: A special rescue version of the Blackhawk is the **HH60G Pave Hawk**. This can be identified by such extra features as an extendable flight refuelling probe and a radome that houses a weather avoidance/ground mapping radar. 92-26470 of the 210th RS Alaska ANG is at its home base of Kulis ANGB, May 2000. This unit also fits skis to the undercarriage for both snow and soft ground landings.

Below: Produced by Eurocopter as an Alouette replacement the **AS350 Ecureuil** is a light multi-purpose helicopter operated by sixteen air arms. **AS350B** E321 of the Ecuadorian Army is at Guayaquil, September 1997.

Above: Known in UK service as the Squirrel, the Ecureuil is operated by the Defence Helicopter Flying School at Shawbury to give basic flying training to pilots from all three services. **Squirrel HT1** ZJ260 is at Fairford, July 1997.

Above: Sikorsky's S64 Skycrane was a heavy lift flying crane helicopter. A pod was designed for the machine to straddle and lift. The Nevada National Guard operates **CH54A Tarhe** 67-18426. It is pictured flying at its Reno-Stead base, September 1988.

Left: The **Bell 206 Jet Ranger** is one of the most popular helicopters on both the civil and military market. US Army use is observation and liaison. **OH58A Kiowa** 71-20554, 51/USNTPS, is on loan to the USN Test Pilots School at Patuxent River, May 1989.

Right: Operated by Esc 3 of the Ecuadorian Navy, **Bell 206B** HN-317 is at its Guayaquil base, September 1997.

Above: Canada has two designations for the Bell 206: CH136 for the OH58A equipped with a 317 shp Allison T63 engine; and CH139 for the 206B equipped with the 400 shp Allison 250. **Bell CH139** 139302 is at Winnipeg, June 1990.

Right: A second contender for the Mi-24 replacement is the **Mi-28** (NATO code-name Havoc). This is another small but heavily armed craft. 014(White) Mi-28N is at Zhukovsky, August 1995. This helicopter is equipped with an under-nose sensor package with forward looking infra-red and low-light TV.

Below: The Hughes 500 was developed from the 369/OH6 light observation helicopter. The type is renowned for its manoeuvrability. Colombian Air Force **Hughes 500E** FAC 4254 is seen being worked on at Gomez AFB, September 1997.

Below: 031(Blue) is a **Kamov Ka-31** (NATO code-name Helix). This variant has a large retractable radar antenna below the fuselage. Its role is that of AEW or radar picket duties aboard a ship. It is pictured at Zhukovsky, August 1995.

Above: The Eurocopter SA366 Dauphin was purchased by the US Coast Guard service as the **HH65A Dolphin**. Its role is short-range rescue from either ship or shore base. 6592 of USCG Detroit is at its Selfridge ANG base, June 1990.

Below: The German Army is the largest user of the **Eurocopter (MBB) Bo105**. With a fleet of 300+ they are used in the role of scout or, as pictured, anti-tank operations. Bo105P 86+83 of PzAbw Reg.16 is at Fassberg, June 1983.

Below: The **Kamov Ka-50** (NATO code-name Hokum) is a heavily armed attack helicopter intended as a Mi-24 replacement. 018 is seen at Zhukovsky, August 1995.

Below: Known as the Hkp9 in Swedish Army service, the **Bo105** is used in the anti-armour role equipped with TOW missiles. 09218 of army unit AF1 is at Fairford, July 1996.

Left: Denmark has operated the big Sikorsky for many years. **S61A** U-280 of Esk 722 is at Lee-on-Solent, July 1972. Its role was SAR.

Below: Known in Canada as the CH124, the Sea King is used for anti-submarine operations. **CH124A** 12437 is at Hamilton, Ont in an all-grey low-visibility scheme, June 1990.

Below: Designed by Sikorsky the **H3/S61 Sea King** has been one of the most popular and widely used helicopters of all time. Seen at Jacksonville NAS, FL, in July 1974, is **SH-3H** 149690 430/AR of HS1. This variant was used by the US Navy for ASW operations. (SGW)

Below: Derived from the civil Sikorsky S62 the HH52 was operated by the US Coast Guard in an SAR role. Powered by a single 1250 shp GE T58 engine, the type was fully amphibious. **HH52A** 1400 from USCG Miami is at its Opa Locka base, October 1981.

Above: Westland licence-build the Sea King and have out-sold their American counterpart. The Royal Navy is the largest UK user, ASW operations being the main role. **Sea King HAS1** XV675 665/PO from 737 Squadron, a Portland-based training unit, is seen at Lee-on-Solent, July 1974.

Above: The **Sea King HC4** is configured for commando operations with the Royal Marines. It has seats for twenty-eight troops together with floor armour. ZD477/Y of 845 Squadron, Royal Navy, is seen in SFOR marking at Fairford, July 1997.

Right: The Falklands War found the Royal Navy in desperate need of an airborne early warning aircraft. The result was the **Sea King AEW2**. This has an inflatable radome that is swung down below the helicopter in flight. Sea King AEW2 XV664 180/CU of 849 Squadron is at Yeovilton, July 1994. The black and white tail marks are to commemorate the fiftieth Anniversary of 'D' Day.

Left: **Sea King HAR5** XV705 821/CU of 771 Squadron is operated in an SAR role. It is seen at Yeovilton, July 1994. The unit is based at Culdrose in Cornwall.

Right: Australia ordered ten Sea Kings in 1972 for anti-submarine duties. Original operations were onboard HMAS *Melbourne*; when this aircraft carrier was scrapped they flew from coastal bases. Sea King Mk50 N16-125 of 817 Squadron, RAN is at Greenham Common, June 1977.

Above: Two Sea Kings are operated by the RAE for trials and test work. Sea King 4X ZB507 is seen in its special colour scheme at Farnborough, September 1988.

Above: Germany was the first export customer for the Westland Sea King. Sea King Mk41 89+71 of German Navy unit MFG3 is at Lee-on-Solent, July 1987. The role of the type was SAR.

Aerobatic teams

Since pilots first flew they have joined with others to fly in formation and to perform aerobatics. This has led to most air arms having some form of display team to represent themselves to the public. They are also used as a form of recruitment or as a sales tool for that nation's aerospace industry. The units following include the full-time professional teams and the 'Friday afternoon' part-timers. Together they make up the most popular of air show attractions.

Left: The Slovak Republic's 'The White Albatross' team is pictured flying the Aero L39 Albatross jet trainer. The team was photographed at Fairford, July 1999.

Below: Since its formation in 1965 the Royal Air Force Aerobatic Team 'The Red Arrows' have been thrilling crowds world-wide with their second-to-none displays. They are pictured with their first mount, the Folland Gnat, at Chivenor, August 1969. From the 1980 season they have flown the BAe Hawk.

Above: Poland's official aerobatic unit are 'The White Iskras' flying the PZL TS11 Iskra trainer. They are seen in close formation at Fairford, July 1995.

Right: The Ukrainian Air Force was only created in 1992. Seen at Fairford are six MiG-29s of 'The Falcons' team, July 1997.

Below: Flying the big long-range Sukhoi Su-27 fighter are 'The Russian Knights'. They are seen at Zhukovsky, August 1995.

Below: Now operating the Northrop F5 the Swiss Air Force aerobatic unit 'Patrouille Suisse' flew the classic Hawker Hunter before the conversion. The team are seen at Boscombe Down with five of their Hunters streaming smoke, June 1992.

Above: Another Russian Air Force team 'The Swifts' fly the MiG-29. They mix both single- and twin-seat aircraft and are seen at Zhukovsky, August 1995.

Left: Despite budget cut backs Russia runs several teams. The L39 Albatross team 'Rus Six' is from the training unit at Vyasma. They are seen at Zhukovsky, August 1995.

Above: Austria operated 'The Silver Birds' team equipped with the SAAB 105 trainer. They are pictured at Greenham Common, July 1976.

Above: The Swedish Air Force 'Team 60' also fly the SAAB 105. The type is known in service as the Sk60. The team is pictured at Fairford, July 1996.

Below: Seven **Northrop F5**s of the Turkish Air Force team 'The Turkish Stars' are seen in tight formation at Fairford, July 1996.

Above: A part-time team from the Irish Air Corps flew the **CM170 Magister** trainer. Known as 'The Swallows' they are seen at Fairford, July 1997.

Left: The Belgian Air Force team '*Diables Rouge*' were disbanded due to budget cut backs. They flew the **CM170 Magister**. The team is pictured ending a display at Lakenheath in August 1975.

Below: Flying the big, heavy **Sukhoi Su-22** in a team cannot be easy. The Czech Air Force unit '*Team Duha*' from Namest put on an excellent display at Fairford, July 1995.

Above: Flying the local built **CASA 101 Aviojet** trainer is the Spanish Air Force aerobatic team '*Patrulla Aguila*'. They are seen landing in formation at Fairford, July 1995.

Left: Portugal's air force team '*Asas de Portugal*' used to fly the **Cessna T37** trainer; they are pictured rolling around Fairford, July 1989.

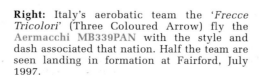

Right: Italy's aerobatic team the '*Frecce Tricolori*' (Three Coloured Arrow) fly the **Aermacchi MB339PAN** with the style and dash associated that nation. Half the team are seen landing in formation at Fairford, July 1997.

Below: Flying four **Alouette III**s the Dutch Air Force operated a team named 'The Grasshoppers'. They are pictured at Fairford, July 1989.

Below: Brazil's aerobatic team fly the locally built **T27 Tucano**. Seen at Abbotsford, BC in August 1986 is the '*Esquadrilha da Fumaca*' (Smoke Squadron) landing in formation.

Above: The USAF team 'The Thunderbirds' fly smartly painted **F16**s. They are pictured at Reno, NV, September 1988.

Above: Unlikely to be seen out of their native Yugoslavia for some years to come is the '*Letece Zvezde*' (Flying Stars) team. They fly the **Soko G4A Super Galeb**. They are pictured at Hradec Králové in the Czech Republic, August 1998. (SGW)

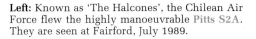

Left: Known as 'The Halcones', the Chilean Air Force flew the highly manoeuvrable **Pitts S2A**. They are seen at Fairford, July 1989.

Above: The US Navy have their own display team 'The Blue Angels'. They are renowned for the tightest formation keeping. Four **F/A18 Hornets** are seen at Patuxent River, MD, May 1989.

Above: The Royal Navy flew a team called 'The Sharks'. It was made up of four **Gazelle HT2**s of 705 Squadron, the type's training unit. They are seen at Boscombe Down, June 1992.

Index